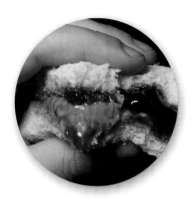

Peanut Butter, Milk, and Other Deadly Threats

What You Should Know About Food Allergies

ISSUES IN FOCUS TODAY

Sherri Mabry Gordon

 Enslow Publishers, Inc.
40 Industrial Road
Box 398
Berkeley Heights, NJ 07922
USA

http://www.enslow.com

To Rachel and Blake.
You are my inspiration.

Copyright © 2006 by Sherri Mabry Gordon

Library of Congress Cataloging-in-Publication Data

Gordon, Sherri Mabry.
    Peanut butter, milk, and other deadly threats : what you should know
    about food allergies / Sherri Mabry Gordon.
        p. cm. — (Issues in focus today)
    Includes bibliographical references and index.
    ISBN-10: 0-7660-2529-2
    1. Food allergy—Juvenile literature. I. Title. II. Series.
    RC596.G67 2006
    616.97'5—dc22

                                                    2005029219
ISBN-13: 978-0-7660-2529-5

Printed in the United States of America

10 9 8 7 6 5 4 3 2

To Our Readers:
We have done our best to make sure all Internet Addresses in this book were active
and appropriate when we went to press. However, the author and the publisher have no
control over and assume no liability for the material available on those Internet sites
or on other Web sites they may link to. Any comments or suggestions can be sent by
e-mail to comments@enslow.com or to the address on the back cover.

Illustration Credits: BananaStock, pp. 3, 5, 58, 99; Scott Bauer, U.S. Dept of
Agriculture/Agricultural Research Service, p. 30; courtesy of Dey L.P., p. 24;
Jack Dykinga, U.S. Department of Agriculture/Agricultural Research Service, pp. 3, 92;
istockphoto.com, pp. 1, 3, 14, 21, 43, 47, 87, 90, 103; PhotoDisc, p. 81; Photos.com,
pp. 3, 17, 26, 36, 43, 49, 54, 60, 67, 71, 72, 76, 78, 95, 97, 101; courtesy of Michelle
Risinger, p. 8.

Cover Illustration: iStock Photos (large illustration and background); Photos.com
(background); BananaStock (small illustration).

C o n t e n t s

Author's Note

The author would like to acknowledge the assistance of the Food Allergy and Anaphylaxis Network and the Food Allergy Initiative.

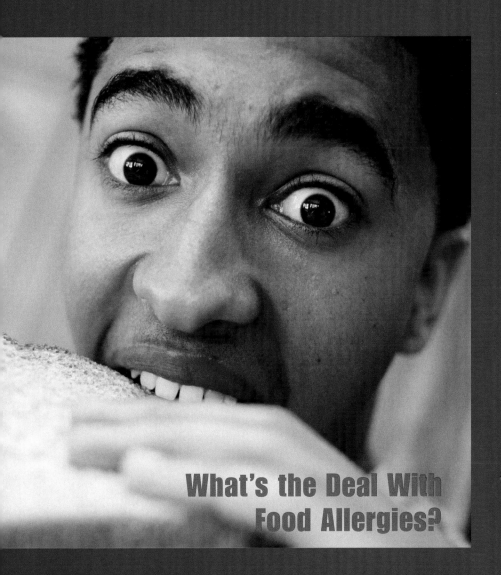

What's the Deal With Food Allergies?

Michelle Risinger was a typical teenager. She loved listening to music and talking on the telephone. She liked to hang out, had chores to do and homework to complete. She even got grounded every now and then.

But there also was something unique about Michelle. She had food allergies (and she still does). Diagnosed when she was two years old with a life-threatening allergy to tree nuts, Michelle did not have her first serious reaction until she was twelve years old.

"I got away without having any serious reactions, in large part, because my parents were so overprotective," Michelle recalls. "I had insignificant reactions, but I never actually ate a nut."

But when Michelle was twelve years old, her mother brought home a box of oatmeal raisin cookies from a party. The ingredients label did not mention nuts, so everyone assumed the cookies were safe for Michelle to eat. Although Michelle's mother had told her that she could not have a cookie, as soon as her mother and her sister left to rent a movie, she ate one anyway. Michelle says:

> My dad was upstairs at the time and as soon as the cookie was in my mouth, my throat instantly closed shut and I knew deep down that I was having a reaction. I definitely knew that something was wrong, but I was only twelve and I had never had a reaction like that before, and I was told not to eat the cookie. So, unfortunately, I waited about ten minutes before I went upstairs to get my dad and I was in a really bad way by that time.

Michelle says her eyes were completely swollen shut, her throat was closing, and she was burning up and itching like crazy:

> What happens is your esophagus closes first and then your trachea starts to close. So my esophagus was completely squeezed shut. I was having trouble swallowing, and [my throat] scratched a lot. And then by the time I went upstairs to get my dad, I was having trouble breathing.

She told her father she had eaten a cookie and that there were no nuts listed in the ingredients, but something was very wrong and that they needed to call 911. She recalls:

> We went back downstairs and I was having trouble thinking by then. I went and got my EpiPen [allergy medication injector] and he called 911 while I gave myself [a shot with] the EpiPen. I remember you're supposed to hold it in your thigh for 10 seconds or so and I think I got up to about 5 and I couldn't remember the next number. I think I ended up holding it in for longer than 10 seconds, because I couldn't remember the numbers that I had counted, and then I passed out on the floor.

While waiting on the front porch of their home for the emergency squad to arrive, Michelle was going in and out of consciousness. She says:

> This will get my dad every time. I remember him looking down at me and I remember thinking this is probably the last time I'm going to see him, and I made myself say, "I love you, Dad." Then I completely passed out and I guess my dad thought that I had died. . . . I remember hearing my dad's voice calling my name, and I remember coming back from that and thinking that he was calling my name to get up for school. As I was starting to refocus again, I remembered that we were out on the porch and then the porch came into focus. That was very bizarre. I mean, I was very close [to dying].

The paramedics later told Michelle's parents that she had about a minute left before cardiac arrest when they arrived. And when her mother, who arrived just as the squad did, asked why they were not transporting Michelle, they replied that she was not stable yet and that they did not think they should move her. After finally arriving at the hospital, Michelle received three doses of epinephrine, lots of Benadryl, and prednisone and other steroids.

"I was there for quite a while and it turns out that the cookie had walnuts in it and they were not listed on the ingredients," Michelle explains. "So that was my first experience and by far the worst, mostly because I waited too long to get my dad."

Today, Michelle attends American University in Washington, D.C. She is still a lot like other girls her age—she likes clothes, worries about her grades, and has high hopes for a future career. But having food allergies has also matured her, making her responsible and levelheaded well beyond her twenty years. Michelle explains:

> It is definitely a big thing when you have your life in your hands at twelve years old, and it could have potentially been taken away. [I] gave myself the EpiPen that saved my life. . . . Your life really is in your hands. I [also] know what it feels like to have your life slipping

For someone like Michelle Risinger with food allergies, a simple mistake in choosing a snack can mean a trip to the emergency room.

away. I think [having food allergies] also made me strong and very independent, and independent minded. I have more experience [with the] potential consequences [of my actions] than my peers do. I feel like people want to experiment in high school and what not, and I sort of know what the consequences will be before I do anything. I feel like I am one step ahead of everybody else, because I think about what would happen in the end.[1]

An Overview of Food Allergies

Imagine how *you* would feel if you suddenly began gasping for breath at a friend's birthday party after taking just one bite of cake. That is exactly what might happen if you had food allergies and ate something you thought was safe.

Under normal circumstances, food usually does not cause a response like that, but with a true food allergy a person's immune system overreacts. (The immune system is the part of the body that protects it from infection, germs, and disease.) During an allergic response to food, ordinarily harmless foods like cow's milk or peanuts are seen as invaders. The body mistakenly believes that it must protect itself from these foods or invaders and reacts. Unfortunately, this reaction harms the body rather than protects it.

In the United States, as many as 11 million people have true food allergies.[2] These people must pay close attention to everything they eat. Just one bite of the wrong food could put them in a life-or-death situation. In fact, an estimated 150 to 200 people die each year from allergic reactions to food. Additionally, an estimated thirty thousand emergency room visits and two thousand hospitalizations annually are caused by food allergies.[3]

When food-allergic individuals come in contact with a food allergen—the protein in a particular food that causes an allergic reaction—they can experience everything from a tingling sensation in the mouth, to swelling of the tongue and throat, to difficulty breathing. They may also experience hives, vomiting, abdominal cramps, diarrhea, a drop in blood pressure, and loss of consciousness. If not treated, they can even die. Symptoms of a food allergy response typically appear within minutes to two hours after a person comes in contact with the food allergen.

Food Allergies and Food Intolerances

People often think that a food intolerance is the same thing as a food allergy, but it is not. Food intolerance is a metabolic disorder and does not affect the immune system. (A metabolic disorder is a disturbance in the body's ability to break down food.) Some people react to common food additives such as food coloring, preservatives, and flavorings. However, unlike food allergies, these reactions do not affect the immune system.

Lactose intolerance is one common example of food intolerance, and it is frequently mistaken for a food allergy. But people with lactose intolerance are not allergic to milk—they just do not have the enzyme (lactase) needed to digest milk sugar. Although their symptoms are uncomfortable and can include gas, bloating, and abdominal pain, they usually are not life threatening like the symptoms of an allergic reaction can be.

Food Allergens

The parts of foods that cause allergic reactions are called food allergens. They are usually proteins. The top eight food allergens are cow's milk, eggs, peanuts, tree nuts, soy, shellfish, fish, and wheat. The allergenic proteins in these foods cause up to 90 percent of all allergic reactions to food.[4]

Foods are grouped into families according to their origin. For example, peanuts, kidney beans, lima beans, and soybeans are all members of the legume family. Crab, lobster, prawns, and shrimp are crustaceans, and belong in the shellfish family. Surprisingly, fish and shellfish are not members of the same food family.

For some foods, especially tree nuts and shellfish, an allergy to one member of a food family may mean that a person is allergic to other foods in the family. This is known as cross-reactivity. On the other hand, a person may be allergic to both peanuts and walnuts, which are from different families. These allergies are called coincidental allergies because they are not related.

Within animal groups of foods, cross-reactivity is not as common. For example, people allergic to cow's milk can usually eat beef, and those allergic to eggs can usually eat chicken. Shellfish such as shrimp, crab, and lobster are most likely to cause an allergic reaction. Mollusk shellfish such as clam and oysters can be allergenic, but reactions are less common.

Food allergies in children and in adults differ somewhat. For example, in children milk, eggs, peanuts, soy, and wheat are the most common allergens. Sometimes children will outgrow allergies to milk, eggs, soy, and wheat, but they are less likely to outgrow allergies to peanuts, tree nuts, fish, and shellfish.[5]

For adults, the most common food allergies are peanuts, tree nuts, fish, eggs,

> **During an allergic response to food, ordinarily harmless foods like cow's milk or peanuts are seen as invaders. The body mistakenly believes that it must protect itself from these invaders and reacts.**

and shellfish. Typically, adults do not lose their allergies. Also, developing food allergies is not limited to childhood. Adults who have never had food allergies can develop them later in life—especially to shellfish.[6]

A Growing Problem

Years ago, food allergies were practically unheard of, although they did exist. Today, though, American classrooms often have at least one food-allergic child in attendance. And the numbers are rising.

In fact, according to a 2004 study released by the American Academy of Allergy, Asthma and Immunology, food allergies are a much bigger health challenge than was once thought. Roughly one in twenty-five Americans is now believed to be affected by one or more food allergies. And the prevalence of peanut allergy in children has doubled over a five-year period, according to a study in the *Journal of Allergy and Clinical Immunology.*

In addition, the study found that while peanuts are often perceived as the most common food allergy, they are not.

What Are the Chances of Having a Food Allergy?

The following is an overview of a person's chances of developing food allergies:

- 6 percent of children younger than three years of age have food allergies.

- 2.5 percent of newborns have a reaction to cow's milk in the first year of life.

- 80 percent of these milk-allergic newborns outgrow their allergies by five years of age.

- 25 percent of the remaining group will continue to have problems until they are age eleven to nineteen.

- 35 percent of newborns with cow's milk allergy will acquire other allergies.

- 1.5 percent are allergic to eggs in childhood.

- 0.5 percent develop allergies to peanuts in early childhood.

- 35 percent of young children with eczema (a dry, scaly rash that itches) have food allergies.

- 6 to 8 percent of young asthma patients have wheezing caused by food allergies.

- 1.1 percent of adults and children are allergic to peanuts and tree nuts.

- 2 percent of American adults have food allergies.

- 85 percent of children with food allergies are allergic to cow's milk, eggs, peanuts, fish, soy, or wheat.[7]

Seafood allergies affect approximately 6.5 million people, while 3 million people have allergies to peanuts or tree nuts.[8]

Food Allergies on the Rise

Why the increase in food allergies? There are a number of theories for the steady increase. The most popular theories include the hygiene theory, early introduction of food allergens, and genetics.

The hygiene theory. One popular explanation is the hygiene theory. Interestingly, the number of people with food allergies is climbing in developed countries such as the United States, Canada, and Great Britain. However, research over the last three decades has shown that this is not the case in less developed countries.

According to Dr. Robert Wood, director of the pediatric allergy clinic at Johns Hopkins Medical Institutions in Baltimore:

> The fewer germs in terms of infection and the environment, the more time the immune system has to worry about things like allergens. Recent studies indicate that growing up in a large family or [attending a] daycare center actually decreases the likelihood of developing an allergy.[9]

Early food introduction. There is a direct link between how early a particular food is given to children and how common the allergy to that food is. For example, in both England and Australia the number of peanut allergies has increased recently. In fact, the number of peanut allergies reported in these countries is almost equal to the number of peanut allergies reported in the United States. The reason is simple: Parents and caregivers are offering younger and younger children food containing peanuts, like the beloved peanut butter and jelly sandwich.[10]

In fact, the more prominent a food is in the food supply, the greater the chances are of people becoming allergic to it. For instance, rice allergy is common in Japan, while fish allergies are one of the most common in Scandinavia.[11]

Genetics. Some children are just more prone to develop food allergies because of their family history. If a family member on either side of the child's family has allergies, then chances are high that the child could have inherited an immune system that is predisposed to developing food allergies—even if other family members have only environmental allergies like hay fever.

One explanation for the rise in food allergies is the introduction of new foods at younger ages.

"Certain families are more likely or prone to have children who develop food allergies," says Dr. Robert S. Zeiger, director of allergy research and clinical professor of pediatrics in San Diego. "Families in which both mother and father, or parent and sibling have allergies are the most susceptible. The inheritance of one's genetic makeup from one's parents is most responsible."[12]

For example, children born into families with a history of allergies of any type are two to four times more likely to develop an allergy as compared to children from families without allergic parents. Additionally, studies have shown that there is a 7 percent chance that a child who has a brother or sister with a peanut allergy will also develop a peanut allergy. This study indicates that there is a predisposition, because the risk for these siblings is about fourteen times as high as the risk of peanut allergy in the general population.[13]

Zeiger also says that identical twins are much more likely than fraternal twins to share a food allergy. "Genes are inherited individually by each child, which may explain in part why one child and not another becomes allergic," he explains. "Different allergen exposure can also affect these differences. Genes, food allergen exposure, infections and other factors may all play a role in developing food allergies."[14]

Food Allergies and Organ Transplants

There is some evidence that it may be possible to not only transplant a person's organs but his or her food allergies as well. According to a 2003 report, a sixty-year-old Australian liver transplant patient had a severe allergic reaction from eating cashews a day after he returned home from the hospital. He had never experienced a nut allergy prior to the transplant.

However, the fifteen-year-old liver donor had a known tree nut and peanut allergy and had in fact died from an allergic reaction to peanuts. Once tested, the transplant patient discovered he now had an allergy to peanuts, cashews, and sesame seeds—the same exact allergies as the donor.

Doctors suspect that because the donor died from an allergic reaction, his liver probably contained antibodies that were transferred to the new owner. Researchers conclude that organ donors may need to be screened for food allergies. This may prevent allergies from being transferred to recipients. Those people receiving organs should also be aware of the potential danger.[15]

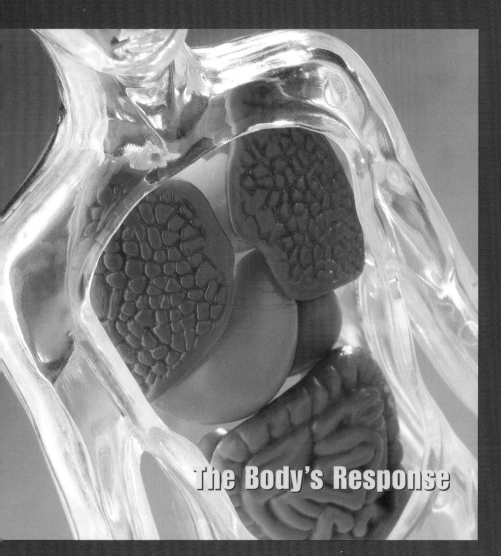

The Body's Response 2

"The second it hits my tongue, I know," says Tracy Thayer, a thirty-eight-year-old mother of four who has asthma and an allergy to peanuts. "The taste is horrible and it just won't go away. Then, there is the itching. It is an uncontrollable itch that goes all the way down your throat. You just want to rip your throat out."

Although Tracy says she would not describe her allergic reaction to peanuts as painful, she says it does hurt and is extremely uncomfortable. "It hurts all the way to your spine. You just feel awful and the taste just won't go away."

Once a reaction begins, Tracy knows that for the next five hours she is going to be severely ill—with swelling, itching, vomiting, and diarrhea. In fact, she will not begin to feel normal again until a day or two later. For that reason, managing her food allergy for most of her life has not been that difficult. "You know how miserable you will feel if you eat it and it just doesn't taste good so you never really want it."

"I've always just looked at [my peanut allergy] as something I have to deal with. I don't consider it a handicap or disability at all," she says. "I've never felt like I was missing out on something."

Because food allergies can run in families, Tracy and her husband, Steve, waited until their kids were five years old before introducing them to peanut products. "They each went to the doctor with a thermos of milk and a Reese's Peanut Butter Cup"—that is, all except her youngest daughter, five-year-old Gabby.

One Christmas Eve several years ago, Gabby got into her older sister's Christmas stocking and took out a piece of candy that contained peanuts. "She immediately started saying 'I don't like it; I don't like it'; so I told her to spit it out. I didn't know that she had eaten something that wasn't hers until I saw her lips had swollen."

Although Tracy says she did not worry much about her own peanut allergy growing up, she says she finds herself worrying a little more about her daughter's safety.

> Back then they didn't prescribe the EpiPen, so I never had one. But now I carry one because of Gabby. I also do what I can to keep her safe like checking the snacks at preschool every day. Still I know that one day she is going to eat peanut by accident and it's not going to be anyone's fault. I am prepared for that day.[1]

Fortunately for Tracy, experience with her own peanut allergy has given her the knowledge she needs to competently and efficiently handle her daughter's allergic reaction someday.

Additionally, she will be able to give her daughter something that other parents of food-allergic children cannot—complete understanding of and empathy for the misery that an allergic reaction to food can cause.

Symptoms of a Food Allergy Reaction

The symptoms and severity of food allergies vary from one person to another. For example, a mildly allergic person may suffer only from a runny nose or sneezing, while those who are highly allergic may experience severe, life-threatening reactions.

Symptoms typically appear within minutes to two hours after the person has come in contact with the food to which he or she is allergic. This contact can occur with touching, breathing, or eating the allergic food.

Currently, the best treatment for a food allergy is strict avoidance of the allergy-causing food. It is the only way to avoid an allergic reaction.

How an Allergic Reaction Works

Before an allergic reaction to food can occur, a person first has to be exposed to the food. Research indicates that a fetus (unborn baby) can be exposed to peanut allergens during pregnancy.[2] If the mother did not eat the food during pregnancy or while breast-feeding, then this first sensitization could occur the first time a very young child eats an egg, a piece of cheese, or a peanut butter sandwich. Or it could happen later in life when an adult who has never had problems before eats a lobster or shrimp dinner. Either way, once exposed, the stage is set for an allergic reaction.

An allergic reaction involves two aspects of the immune system response. One is the production of immunoglobulin E (IgE) antibodies, a type of protein that circulates through the blood and protects the body from germs and infection. The other is the mast cell, a specific blood cell that is found in body tissues, especially the nose, throat, lungs, skin, and gastrointestinal tract. The mast cell produces histamines. In general, allergic people have inherited an immune system that makes increased amounts of IgE.

During a food-allergic reaction, the body's immune system mistakenly believes that a harmless substance, in this case a food, is unsafe. In an attempt to protect the body, the immune system creates IgE antibodies to that food. These antibodies attach themselves to the mast cells in the tissues.

Symptoms typically appear within minutes to two hours after the person has come in contact—through touching, breathing, or eating—with the food to which he or she is allergic.

When the allergic person eats the food, the food attaches itself to the antibody. This causes the mast cell to explode and release massive amounts of histamines and other chemicals throughout the body. Histamines are a type of chemical responsible for allergic symptoms that can affect the respiratory system, gastrointestinal tract, skin, and cardiovascular system.

As the mast cells begin releasing histamines and several other chemicals, they are also busy making more. Meanwhile, the food-allergic person is starting to feel ill.

According to *The Parents' Guide to Food Allergies*:

> Any of us who've had a cold or sneezed when the trees began to bud have experienced this type of reaction. It is the same combination of histamine plus other chemical products that gives us the sneezing, runny-nose, itchy-eye misery of colds and hay fever. That's why antihistamines are our first line of defense when it comes to treating cold and allergy symptoms.[3]

Mast cells are usually found in the skin, mucous membranes, lungs, and gastrointestinal tract. Basically, mast cells are waiting to react in the body parts used to eat, to touch, and to breathe. For this reason, food-allergic reactions generally include hives (skin), swollen lips and tongue (mucous membranes), difficulty breathing and wheezing (lungs), vomiting and diarrhea (gastrointestinal tract), or a combination of these symptoms.[4]

Everyone has mast cells located throughout his or her body. But different groups of mast cells are triggered by different allergens. Some mast cells will respond to cow's milk, while others are sensitive to bee stings.

Additionally, wherever the mast cells are triggered, that is where the allergic reaction will show up. For this reason, three different kids, all of them allergic to tree nuts, may react in three very different ways. One child may have most of her mast cells triggered in her skin and get hives. Another may have most of her mast cells triggered in her lungs and have difficulty breathing, and the third child may have most of his cells triggered in the gastrointestinal tract and vomit. The only difference is where the largest number of mast cells is activated.

Each food allergen has its own specific mast cell that seems to react only to that particular food, and those mast cells are not equally distributed throughout the body. As a result, an allergic person can react in different ways

Histamines released by the mast cells are responsible for allergic reactions, including the sniffling and sneezing experienced by those with pollen allergies. Shown are pollen molecules.

to different foods. For example, a boy who gets asthma from peanuts may break out in hives from milk. The peanut-triggered mast cells are mostly in his airway while the milk-triggered mast cells are mostly in his skin.

In the most severe situations, a person will have an allergic reaction in several parts of the body at one time. For example, a person may experience hives, difficulty breathing, and lowered blood pressure.

Anytime more than one part of the body is affected, the reaction is severe, or there is difficulty breathing, doctors call the reaction anaphylaxis.

A Closer Look at Anaphylaxis

Anaphylaxis is the most frightening aspect of food allergies. It is also the most problematic allergic reaction, usually coming on quickly with a severe and sometimes fatal outcome.

Anaphylaxis is a generalized allergic reaction that involves many systems of the body, including the heart, lungs, kidneys, and blood vessels.[5] During anaphylaxis, capillaries dilate and muscles contract. This may result in a drop in blood pressure, difficulty breathing, slowing or stopping of the heart, and possible kidney shutdown.

The word *anaphylaxis* was coined in 1902. Scientists were trying to immunize dogs against a poison by giving them small doses of it. But when the dogs got the poison again, they died suddenly. Because the word *prophylaxis* means protection by immunization, scientists coined the word *anaphylaxis* to mean the opposite of protection. The dogs' deaths helped the scientists understand that the same thing can happen in humans.[6]

During anaphylaxis, blood vessels dilate and begin to leak fluid into the surrounding tissues, producing swelling. The loss of fluid from blood vessels causes a drop in blood pressure, and the person may feel light-headed and even lose consciousness.

Most people experiencing anaphylaxis first sense a feeling of foreboding—their body just does not feel "right"—just before the symptoms appear. Here is how some people felt during an anaphylactic reaction:

- Tiffany, age nine, says: "In mild cases my mouth tastes funny. I get itchy around the mouth and lips and it comes up in spots with swelling. In severe cases I vomit, swell up, can't breathe and have an uncontrollable itch all over my body."[7]

- A mother of a fifteen-year-old boy says her son's lips, tongue, and throat swell. "There also is a tightening of the throat and then he goes unconscious."[8]

- A mother of a seven-year-old boy says: "When he has ingested the offending food, he will start to cough, produce lots of phlegm, swell up in the face, vomit— and without medication, stop breathing."[9]

Peanuts, tree nuts, shellfish, fish, milk, and eggs are the foods most likely to cause anaphylactic reactions. Only a trace amount of a problem food can cause a reaction in some people. Additionally, a recent study of fatal food allergy-induced anaphylaxis showed that adolescents who have peanut or tree nut allergy and asthma and do not have easy access to epinephrine (the drug used

Food-Dependent Exercise-Induced Anaphylaxis

Another form of anaphylaxis is called food-dependent exercise-induced anaphylaxis. This reaction, which is very rare, occurs only when a person eats a specific food and exercises within three to fours hours after eating. Usually, people who have this type of reaction also have other allergies and asthma. Any food can contribute to this type of anaphylaxis, but foods that have been reported include celery, milk, wheat, fruit, shellfish, and fish.

Food-dependent exercise-induced anaphylaxis appears to be twice as common in women as in men. It is also common in people who are in their late teens to thirties.

to treat anaphylaxis) during a reaction are at highest risk for dying.[10]

Some people have a reaction and the symptoms go away only to return two to three hours later. When this happens, it is called a biphasic reaction. Many times the symptoms occur in the respiratory tract and take the individual by surprise.

How Anaphylaxis Is Treated

Epinephrine, which is adrenaline, is the drug of choice in treating anaphylaxis. It helps to prevent the progression of the reaction and reverses the symptoms.

Epinephrine is a prescription drug that is available in injectable form. The most frequently prescribed version in the United States is the EpiPen or EpiPen Jr., which is for children. Because the EpiPen is an auto-injector (a disposable, prefilled automatic injection device), food-allergic people can inject themselves and save their own lives. To do so, they remove the safety cap of the pen and jab it firmly into the thigh and hold it for ten seconds. After doing so, they call for an ambulance. The EpiPen should be given as soon as the symptoms of anaphylaxis are detected.

Once injected, epinephrine acts quickly to constrict blood vessels. It also relaxes the muscles in the lungs to make breathing easier and stimulates the heart-beat. Swelling also stops when epinephrine is injected. Because the effects of the drug wear off in ten to twenty minutes, the person sometimes needs a second injection. As a result, it is extremely important to get to the emergency room as quickly as possible.

Antihistamines, such as Benadryl, and steroids are often used to further improve recovery. Although antihistamines and asthma medications can be used with

This is an EpiPen, an injector containing epinephrine.

epinephrine, they cannot reverse some of the symptoms the way epinephrine can. People who have had epinephrine prescribed must carry it with them at all times, because no one can predict when a reaction will occur.

For Michelle Risinger, who has had more anaphylactic episodes than she cares to remember, carrying the EpiPen is a must. She says that with each of her reactions she has less and less time to react. If she eats something with a tree nut in it, her life is at risk almost immediately.

Overall, she describes anaphylaxis as very uncomfortable. She explains:

> The first reaction is your esophagus closing, which is the scratchy feeling. Then, at least in my case, I get really hot and I feel taut, which is the swelling over my body. I feel like a sausage, like I'm going to explode, like I'm pushed to bigger than I should be. And then when your trachea starts closing, it doesn't hurt, but the fear is what hurts.
>
> Then, your breath starts coming shorter and by the time you get to the point where you're going in and out of consciousness, that's when your chest starts to hurt. But, again, you're so scared at that point that you know it hurts, but that's not what you're thinking about. [Anaphylaxis] is not like a sharp pain like you've been stabbed or anything like that, it's just you're uncomfortable all over.[11]

Food Allergy Testing

"From the time my daughter Rebecca was three weeks old I knew something wasn't quite right," says Sarah Morgan, a thirty-seven-year-old mother of two. "Every time she nursed she would throw her head back, scream, and draw her legs up. It was as if my milk was poison to her."

After watching Rebecca nurse, the family's pediatrician at the time diagnosed her with acid reflux. (This is a condition in which the stomach acids come up and cause a burning sensation.) The doctor prescribed medication that was supposed to make her feel better.

"When the medication did not work, the doctor increased the dose and told me to come back if her condition did not improve," explains Sarah. "But there was still no improvement. And so the cycle began of trying to determine what was wrong with my baby."

Sarah says that in an effort to try to determine what was causing her baby so much pain, she talked to friends, the nurse-midwife who delivered the baby, and several lactation consultants. A number of people mentioned the possibility of a dairy allergy, because what a mother eats is passed through the breast milk to the baby. But every time Sarah mentioned it to the pediatrician, the doctor would brush it off.

"She even suggested that babies could not be accurately diagnosed with allergies at such a young age," she says. "However, she did indicate that Rebecca might do better on formula rather than being breast-fed."

Sarah explains:

After six months of dealing with a fussy baby that didn't sleep well, I finally decided to try formula. Because she would not drink the soy formula, I tried a milk-based formula. Rebecca took the bottle peacefully and actually seemed to like it. Then I removed the bottle and the area around her mouth was covered with hives. I was scared to death as I handed her to my husband and called the pediatrician. By the time the doctor was on the phone, the baby was projectile vomiting.

Although the pediatrician now agreed that Rebecca had a milk allergy, she did not refer us to an allergist for testing or give us much advice on how to handle a milk allergy. It wasn't until Rebecca was eighteen months old that we finally found a pediatrician that would give us the referral we needed to have Rebecca tested by an allergist.

Following Rebecca's allergy tests, the Morgans learned that their daughter had severe allergies to milk and eggs and a slight allergy to peanuts. Additionally, she was allergic to cats, mold, and dust mites. Rebecca was prescribed an antihistamine and epinephrine.

Sarah says:

> What we discovered the day of Rebecca's allergy test was life-changing. But it also was overwhelming and I left the office feeling numb. That afternoon while Rebecca took her nap I cried the entire time. I was angry with the first pediatrician and frustrated that I had not done more. I felt guilty for what I ate while nursing her. But, mostly I mourned the loss of normalcy. The next day, though, I got up with a sense of determination. I was going to learn everything I could about food allergies and I was going to give my daughter the most normal life I could—in spite of her food allergies.[1]

As Sarah learned, it is crucial to the food-allergic person's health, safety, and well-being to get a food allergy properly diagnosed. By doing so, appropriate medications can be prescribed and the patient (or the patient's parents) can be educated about how to read food labels and how to effectively avoid the food allergens to which the individual is allergic.

Typically, a board-certified allergist is the best-qualified source for diagnosing a food allergy even if the person has had a serious reaction. A board-certified allergist is a doctor who has undergone three years of training in either internal medicine or pediatrics, followed by another two to three years in the field of allergy and clinical immunology. An allergist must renew the allergy certification every ten years.[2]

Diagnosing a food allergy requires a carefully organized and detailed assessment of the problem. The purpose of food allergy testing is to determine in a reliable manner to which food allergens a person is allergic. When used with a complete patient history and a food diary, food allergy tests can be very accurate and useful tools. (A food diary is a log listing the foods a person eats, the date and time, and any symptoms he or she experiences.) The two most common methods of food allergy testing are skin tests and blood tests. However, there is a third test known as the food challenge that is extremely useful in diagnosing food allergies.

Skin Tests

For a skin test, the allergist prepares a tray of food extracts to use in testing. Usually the extracts include the most common food allergens (milk, egg, peanut, soy, tree nut, wheat, fish, shellfish) plus any other foods the person may have trouble with. For example, if the person has had symptoms when eating corn, it would be included in the test.

Unfortunately, a person cannot accurately be tested for a food that he or she has never been exposed to. Examples of exposure include having eaten the food at least once or being a breast-fed child whose mother ate the food. For example, a two-year-old who has never eaten shrimp could not be tested for a shellfish allergy.

In most cases, skin tests are performed on the person's back. A checkerboard pattern is drawn on the person's skin to show where each food extract will be placed. A small drop of food extract is placed within each square and then pricked with a needle. If the patient has a history of anaphylaxis, then the allergist might instead place a drop of that particular food extract on the person's arm.

A positive skin test indicates the presence of IgE antibodies. In a positive test, a hive will develop in reaction to the food or foods the person is allergic to. A hive, which looks like a mosquito bite, is called a wheal by allergists. The red area surrounding the hive is referred to as the flare.

Typically, the hive appears within minutes of the test and feels very itchy, just like a mosquito bite. A negative result to the skin test means there are no IgE antibodies, and a hive will not appear.

Because everyone's skin may react to a skin test in a different way, allergists often include a planned positive reaction and a planned negative reaction in the test. In other words, they knowingly prick the skin with two substances—one that they know will get a positive result and one that they know will get a negative result. Then they are able to use the planned reactions to identify which marks on the person's skin are only skin irritations and which marks are allergic reactions.

Generally, the solution used to dilute the allergen, also known as a diluent, is used to produce the negative test result at one prick site. Meanwhile, a histamine solution is used to produce a true allergic reaction (or positive test result) at another prick site.

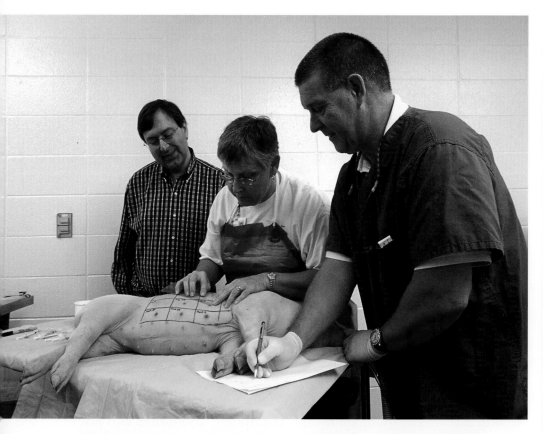

These researchers at the University of Arkansas are doing an allergy test on a pig with soybean sensitivity. The test is similar to that used for humans.

When interpreting the skin test, many allergists use a scale of 1+ up to 4+ to describe (or measure) the size of the hives. For example, a person may have a 3+ reaction to eggs, a 4+ reaction to milk, and a 2+ reaction to peanuts. Naturally, you might assume that because the hive for milk was a 4+, the person's reaction to milk would be severe. In some cases this might be true, but it is not always the case.

Food allergies are very unpredictable. For instance, someone with only a 2+ hive to a certain food may become extremely ill from just one bite, while someone with a 4+ hive may have only a minor reaction. One possible explanation is the location of the mast cells. Obviously a person with mast cells triggered primarily in the skin will have bigger hives. However, they may not get as sick from a certain food as someone who has a lot of mast cells triggered in the lungs or digestive tract, but has smaller hives during a skin test.

Overall, the skin prick test is considered highly accurate. It is extremely rare for people to test negative (or get no hive at all) to the food and then have an allergic reaction after eating it. Conversely, patients do sometimes have some false positives. For example, it is not uncommon for someone to test positive to a food in the same family as the food they are truly allergic to. One example is a peanut-allergic child who tests positive to soy. This happens because the allergenic proteins of peanut and soy are so similar. The allergist would consider the patient's past history before stating that the person is allergic to soy, especially if the person has been eating soy with no problems.

Blood Tests

The blood test that is usually given to patients to check for food allergies is called a RAST, which stands for radioallergosorbent test. In general, the test measures the blood to determine the amount (or level) of IgE antibodies present. The RAST can be used to predict the likelihood of a food allergy.

After the blood samples are taken from the patient, they are sent to a laboratory to be tested. Once at the lab, the blood is placed on absorbent disks that contain specific food proteins. Then the amount of IgE antibodies produced in response to the specific foods is measured.

Each food has a unique measurement or number that is used to predict whether or not the person has a food allergy. When the IgE antibody levels are greater than the pre-established values, there is greater than a 95 percent chance that the person will have some type of allergic reaction.[3] Lower levels may also indicate a potential allergic reaction. With lower values, the allergist will also consider the patient's history before making a recommendation.

One benefit of a RAST that is performed every few years is that it may indicate whether or not the child's antibody levels are dropping. If the levels are dropping, the child could be outgrowing the allergy.

Doctors usually prefer conducting a skin test to test for food allergies rather than a blood test because it is simpler, less expensive, and more readily available. One exception is that if the patient has a history of severe life-threatening reactions to a food, a RAST is less risky than a skin test.

There are also other uses for blood tests. A recent report indicates that blood tests can also be used to help allergists determine when to reintroduce a food that a child has been allergic to. The report provides guidelines for using antibody levels to decide if the child is ready for a third type of food allergy test—an oral food challenge.

"These findings make it clear that doing a blood test to measure IgE levels can accurately predict how a patient will fare during a food challenge," says Dr. Robert Wood, a pediatric allergist at the Johns Hopkins Children's Center. A food challenge consists of giving small amounts of the allergen to the patient to see if a reaction occurs. "We recommend routine use [of blood tests] to screen children with suspected allergies before a food challenge is performed."

Wood adds that doctors can use information from the blood test as a guideline to decide when foods can be reintroduced into a child's diet. Until recently, such information was not readily available. As a result, there was a lot of uncertainty about when to do a food challenge.

"Without a diagnosis from a food challenge, children with low IgE levels who may no longer be allergic, or who were misdiagnosed with a food allergy, may be unnecessarily avoiding foods like milk, eggs and peanuts which have significant nutritional benefits," Wood says.[4]

In some cases, the allergist will order both a skin test and a blood test before diagnosing a food allergy. When both the skin test and the blood test come back positive for a certain food, the answer is clear. However, sometimes a skin test will be positive (regardless of whether or not a true food allergy exists) while the RAST is inconclusive. Then, there is only one way to find the answer—by conducting an oral food challenge.

Oral Food Challenges

The food challenge is the only test that can determine a person's allergies once and for all. It is often called the gold standard for food allergy testing. Basically, the test consists of feeding a person small amounts of foods.

One form of food challenge is called the double-blind placebo-controlled food challenge. It is performed under strictly controlled conditions. "Double-blind" means that neither the patient nor the person who is giving the food knows what allergen (if any) is offered at each "taste test." "Placebo-controlled" means that not every taste test has an allergenic substance. Sometimes the test has a placebo—a harmless non-allergenic food substance. And "food challenge" simply means offering a possible food allergen to someone.

The reason this test is double-blind is to rule out any psychological reactions. For instance, a girl who believes she is allergic to milk and fears a reaction could have difficulty breathing and vomit when fed milk. The problem is that those symptoms could come from anxiety and not from an immune system response. The same is true with the health care worker. He or she may be nervous about feeding the food allergen and so may cause the patient to become nervous. For this reason, only those preparing the tests know what is in the test foods.

> The food challenge—feeding a person small amounts of foods and watching for a reaction—is the only test that can determine a person's allergies once and for all.

The placebo-controlled portion of the test helps differentiate the psychological responses from the immune system responses. So a person who complains about nausea after taking the placebo food is most likely reacting to the idea of the test and not the test.

The food challenge portion is ultimately testing the person's immune system by offering a possible food allergen. Sometimes when skin tests are negative and the person is believed to have outgrown the allergy, the allergist may suggest challenging the person with the food at home. In the case of a child, the allergist tells the parent exactly how much of the food should be offered and how many times a day. As long as the rules are followed everything is usually just fine. Food challenges at home should only be conducted if the doctor says it is safe. Usually, food challenges at home are reserved for children who had only minor reactions to food allergens.

Outgrowing a Food Allergy

Within the first three to five years of life, approximately 85 percent of children with food allergies lose their sensitivity to common allergy-causing foods, including eggs, milk, soy, and wheat. In the remaining 15 percent, there is still a slight chance that they will develop tolerance.[5] Although allergies to peanuts, tree nuts, and shellfish are often considered lifelong, there is no age at which one can be sure that they will always exist.

For example, peanut allergy has usually been seen as permanent. But researchers have found that 18 to 21 percent of children in their studies outgrew the allergy.[6] Additionally, studies have found many instances in which the skin test to a food remains positive for a long time after actual tolerance has developed.[7] What this research suggests is that food challenges play an important role in determining if a food allergy has been outgrown.

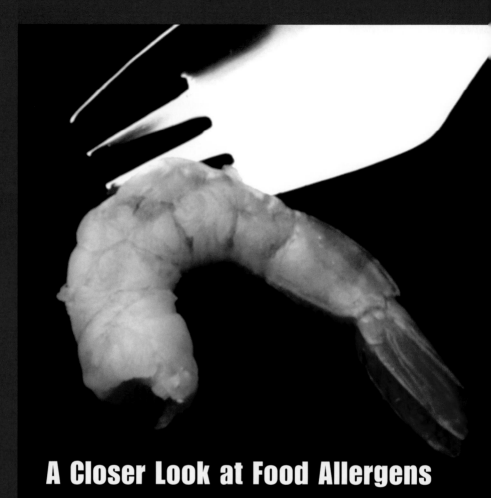

A Closer Look at Food Allergens

"What is food to one man may be fierce poison to others" is an old saying that certainly describes food allergens to a tee. While most people view eating specific foods as a way to be healthy— for example, drinking milk builds strong bones and teeth—for the truly food-allergic person, certain foods can be poison and can have the power to kill.

Although the foods that cause allergies are all unique, they do have something in common: They contain a large protein, called a glycoprotein.[1] For the most part, the allergenic properties are not affected by heat, digestion, food processing, or enzymes.

(Enzymes are proteins that break down components of food so that they can be used by the body.) For this reason, a major food allergen (milk, peanut, shellfish, fish, tree nut, egg, soy, wheat) in any form—natural, cooked, or processed—can cause symptoms in a sensitized person. To better understand food allergies, it is important to understand a little more about the major food allergens.

Milk Allergies

Although peanut allergies get the most media attention, more children in the United States and throughout the world have allergic reactions to milk than have reactions to any other food.[2] In fact, 2 to 3 percent of children have a milk allergy in the first two years of life.[3] In addition, nearly 25 percent of these infants remain sensitive into the second decade of life, and 35 percent develop other allergies.[4]

These reactions are mostly to cow's milk, but allergic individuals will react to goat's milk and mare's milk as well. Breast-fed babies with allergies are not actually allergic to their mother's milk, but to something in the mother's diet, such as peanut butter, milk products, or eggs. Everything a breast-feeding mother eats and drinks is passed through the breast milk to the baby in small quantities.

There are many proteins in cow's milk, but the two main parts of milk are casein and whey. Casein is the curd that forms when milk sours; whey is the watery part left when the curd is removed. Eighty percent of the protein in milk is casein; whey makes up the remaining 20 percent. Casein is the major allergen in cheese. The harder cheese is, the more casein it has. Whey, on the other hand, consists of two main allergenic proteins— alpha-lactalbumin and beta-lactaglobulin.[5]

In addition to cow's milk, people with a milk allergy must avoid cheese, yogurt, and butter. Margarine, cookies, cakes, and breads can also contain milk. For example, if the food is processed or from a box mix, the ingredients often contain milk in the form of casein, whey, nonfat dry milk, and so on. Many times, homemade versions also contain milk that is either added to the mixture or added in the form of butter or yogurt.

Because a large number of products contain milk, it is important for milk-allergic people to read product labels carefully. Milk protein may be present where it is least expected. For example, many processed meats like sausage, hot dogs, pepperoni, and salami contain milk. Milk is used as a binder to hold the meats together. Additionally, many products marked "nondairy" still contain casein, which will cause a reaction in a milk-allergic individual. Soy cheeses, whipped topping, and nondairy creamer are all examples of products that potentially contain milk protein.

For milk-allergic people, total avoidance of milk and milk products is not only the key to good health but it also provides the best chance of eventually outgrowing the allergy. In fact, about 80 percent of milk-allergic children outgrow their allergy by their fifth birthday.[6]

Total avoidance of milk and milk products provides the best chance of eventually outgrowing a milk allergy.

Currently, new blood tests are being developed that should be able to show whether someone will outgrow a milk allergy and whether he or she is likely to tolerate milk as an ingredient in baked goods in small amounts. In addition, future research should enable allergists to diagnose most milk-allergic patients with blood tests and provide new vaccines that will cure and eventually prevent these allergies.[7]

It is important to point out that people with a milk allergy are not lactose intolerant, and vice versa. Unlike a milk allergy, lactose intolerance does not affect the immune system. Also, people who are lactose intolerant do not always have to avoid

Physical Signs of Milk Allergy

Some young children who are allergic to milk also show some or all of these physical signs (in addition to the typical symptoms of an allergy):

- allergic "shiners" (dark blue, black, or reddish circles under the eyes)
- reddish earlobes
- a reddened nose (from rubbing the tip).[8]

milk. Sometimes they can use lactose-reduced or lactose-free products or take a tablet containing the lactase enzyme (the enzyme lactose intolerant people are missing) before eating dairy foods and be just fine. These steps will do nothing for the milk-allergic individual.

One interesting fact is that there does not seem to be any correlation between milk allergy and lactose intolerance. Kids with milk allergies now are no more likely than the rest of the population to become lactose intolerant. In fact, about 80 percent of the general population lacks the lactase enzyme to some degree. This enzyme is needed to digest lactose (milk sugar). Without enough lactase, a person can become lactose intolerant.[9]

Peanut Allergies

Though people often assume a peanut is a nut, it really is a vegetable that grows in the ground and is a member of the legume family. In addition to peanuts, the legume family includes soybeans, lentils, peas, chickpeas, black-eyed peas, lima beans, kidney beans, and green beans.

Peanuts are both potent and complex, and they contain as many as thirty different proteins. But scientists suspect that only seven of the proteins, and perhaps even fewer, cause allergic reactions.[10] Many believe one reason for their potency is the fact that the proteins found in peanuts are extremely stable. This means that unlike other proteins, peanut proteins are not affected by cooking, chewing, or being exposed to saliva and stomach acid. Research is being conducted to determine which peanut proteins trigger an allergic reaction and why the reaction can vary in severity among allergy sufferers.

Typically, peanut allergies have been viewed as permanent. Recent studies, however, suggest otherwise. For example, a study released in 2003 that was conducted by Dr. David Fleischer and colleagues from Johns Hopkins University School of Medicine showed that peanut-allergic individuals have a 50 percent chance of outgrowing the allergy if they meet certain criteria, such as a low IgE blood level. Experts previously believed that the likelihood of outgrowing a peanut allergy was only 20 percent.[11]

Although a rare occurrence, there are some cases in which a peanut allergy was outgrown but then returned to the person. This happened to three boys who were originally diagnosed with a peanut allergy as babies. As time passed, they became less sensitive to peanuts and were given a food challenge. They passed the food challenge and were able to eat peanuts without having a reaction.

But after passing the food challenge, the boys rarely ate peanuts or food containing peanuts. If they did eat peanut products, it was only in small quantities. This type of eating pattern is believed to sensitize a person to a food. To build tolerance to a food, doctors recommend eating small amounts frequently or large amounts infrequently.[12]

After peanut-allergic individuals pass a food challenge, experts now recommend that they eat peanut products often and carry epinephrine indefinitely. If the doctor and the patient feel that ongoing peanut tolerance has been established, he or she may no longer need to carry epinephrine.[13]

Peanut Allergy at a Glance

The amount of reported cases of peanut allergy doubled from 1997 to 2002, according to one study.

- Allergies to peanuts are responsible for nearly one hundred deaths and fifteen thousand visits to emergency rooms—about half the deaths and emergency room visits caused by all food allergies each year.

- FAAN (Food Allergy and Anaphylaxis Network) estimates that nearly six hundred thousand children in the United States, or about 1 in 125, have a peanut allergy.

- Peanut allergies are reported by more than 1.5 million Americans.

- An amount as small as 1/100 of a peanut can cause a life-threatening reaction in some people.

- A 1988 study of 122 peanut-allergic children showed that 56 percent experienced two cases of accidental ingestion over a 5.4-year period. Most cases occurred outside the home.[14]

Shellfish and Fish Allergies

Seafood is a popular part of the U.S. diet and includes fish such as cod, salmon, and tuna and shellfish such as shrimp, crab, lobster, squid, scallops, clams, and mussels. Allergies to seafood affect approximately 6.5 million people. This number is more than double the number of people who deal with peanut and tree nut allergies.[15]

In fact, a recent study shows that a shellfish allergy is reported by 1 in 50 people and a fish allergy is reported by 1 in 250.[16] However, fish and shellfish are not related in terms of food families, so an allergy to one does not necessarily ensure an allergy to the other.

While most food allergies develop in young children and disappear as they grow older, seafood allergies frequently remain throughout adulthood. In fact, many people first develop seafood allergies as adults. Overall, allergies to seafood tend to be severe and lifelong.

Tree Nut Allergies

Like other food allergies, allergies to nuts often begin during the first years of life. And because nuts are so common—and often hidden ingredients in other foods—it is hard to avoid them. As a result, accidental ingestions with severe reactions are common.

Yet a nut allergy is notoriously unpredictable. A patient may not always have the same kind of reaction each time contact is made with an allergen. Even people who have only experienced minor symptoms may in the future be at risk of suffering a severe anaphylactic reaction.

Nuts grow on trees and include:

- hazelnuts
- pistachios
- Brazil nuts
- cashews
- macadamia nuts
- chestnuts
- almonds
- pecans
- walnuts

However, different nuts can belong to different food families. For example, almonds are in the same food family as peaches, while cashews are in the same family as mangos. But it is not uncommon for people to be allergic to more than one type of nut.

Egg Allergies

Egg allergies are common in infancy and childhood—especially in infants with eczema. Eczema, also known as atopic dermatitis, is a dry scaly skin rash that causes intense itching. About 80

The top eight food allergens—cow's milk, eggs, peanuts, tree nuts, soy, shellfish, fish, and wheat—account for up to 90 percent of all allergic reactions to food.

percent of children with egg allergy will develop a respiratory allergy and asthma.[17]

Eggs are made up of twenty different proteins. Two proteins—ovamucoid and ovalbumin—are primarily responsible for allergic reactions.[18] The egg white is actually more allergenic than the egg yolk. Most egg-allergic people are allergic to the white. However, people who are allergic to egg yolk are often also allergic to chicken, turkey, and other poultry.

The egg white is made mostly of ovalbumin, which is changed by heating and cooking. However, about 4 percent is ovamucoid, which is the most allergenic part and is not affected by heat.[19]

Frequently, egg allergies are outgrown. The odds of outgrowing the allergy improve with total avoidance.

Soy Allergies

Like peanuts, soybeans are legumes. However, a soy allergy rarely causes anaphylaxis like its cousin. Soy allergy is most common in infants. Typically, by three months of age, the allergy is recognizable. In addition, an estimated 43 percent of babies allergic to milk develop a soy allergy when given soy formula.[20]

However, most babies outgrow the allergy by the time they are two. Although adults can be allergic to soy, it is unusual.[21] An allergy to soy protein is similar to milk allergy. Like cow's milk, soy also frequently causes eczema as well as typical allergy symptoms.

Soy by itself is not a common part of the traditional Western diet, but it may surprise some people to realize that as a country we eat large amounts of soy when we eat manufactured foods. In fact, it can be very difficult to avoid soy entirely. Soy increases the nutrient value and adds flavor, so it is a popular ingredient in many convenience foods.

Wheat Allergies

Perhaps the most difficult food allergen to avoid is wheat. Although it is not as common or severe as some other food allergies, it can be one of the most challenging food allergies to deal with. For one thing, wheat is a regular part of our diet, and it is hard to find substitutions for it.

Although grains like wheat contain a lot of carbohydrates, it is still the protein in wheat that causes the immune system response.[22] Wheat and wheat products are often found in foods that we least expect. In addition to bread, cereals, cookies, and cakes, wheat is sometimes found in candy, soup, and even processed cheese.

Oral Allergy Syndrome

People with hay fever may experience what is known as oral allergy syndrome when they eat fresh fruits or vegetables. With oral allergy syndrome, they experience an itchy mouth or scratchy throat caused by raw fruits or vegetables. Cooked or canned foods and juices are usually tolerated.

Basically, oral allergy syndrome is a condition in which the allergic person's body cannot tell the difference between fresh fruits and vegetables and the pollens that cause hay fever. This confusion occurs because the makeup of the foods is similar to that of the pollen.

Although this reaction is an allergic response, it is not life threatening. The symptoms usually resolve within minutes after the food is swallowed or removed from the mouth. Typically, treatment is not necessary.

There are several common pollen-food associations. However, not every person allergic to pollen develops symptoms with cross-reacting fruits or vegetables. Some potential associations include the following:

- An allergy to birch could cause an oral reaction to apple, carrot, peach, plum, cherry, pear, almond, and hazelnut.

Gluten Intolerance vs. Wheat Allergy

Many people believe that a wheat allergy and gluten intolerance are the same thing, but they are not. Gluten intolerance (also called celiac sprue) is a lifelong disease. It is not an allergy. Instead, people with the disorder have an intolerance for gluten, which is a complex mixture of proteins found in grains such as wheat, rye, and barley.

The disease commonly shows up in early childhood with severe symptoms, including chronic diarrhea, abdominal distension, and failure to thrive. (Children who fail to thrive do not grow as expected because they do not take in enough calories or because their bodies do not retain or do not make use of the calories they do take in.)[23] Like food allergies, there is no cure or medicine a person can take to make gluten intolerance go away. People who have a gluten intolerance must strictly avoid gluten in their diets.

- An allergy to grasses could cause an oral reaction to tomato.
- An allergy to ragweed could cause an oral reaction to melons, zucchini, cucumber, kiwi, and banana.[24]

Hidden Allergens and Cross Contact

Carefully reading food labels and checking ingredients is crucial to avoiding a food-allergic reaction. But it is not always enough. Sometimes food-allergic people have to go one step further to protect themselves.

Food allergens have been known to show up in the oddest places—places that might never be expected. One example is the nineteen-year-old college student who knew she was allergic to peanuts. She died in a restaurant after eating just a few bites of chili that was made with peanut butter. Apparently the chef had used peanut butter to thicken the dish.[25]

For this reason, people with food allergies have to think about and question everything they eat. This includes calling food

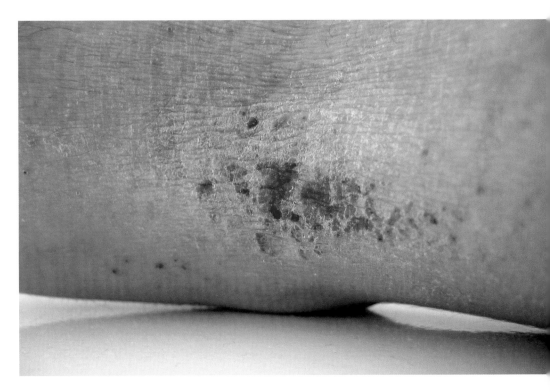

Eczema, characterized by red, itchy skin, is often found among people with allergies to milk, eggs, and soy.

manufacturers, quizzing restaurant staff, and asking lots of questions about how the food was prepared and what it contains.

There is also the issue of cross contact to consider. Cross contact is when one food comes in contact with another food and their proteins mix. Consequently, each food then contains small amounts of the other food, even though it cannot be seen. This small amount of food is enough to potentially cause an allergic reaction. Some examples of ways in which cross contact can happen include:

- When different foods are processed or made on the same equipment by a manufacturer. An example would be a peanut butter cookie made on the same machine as a sugar cookie. Even though the machine may be thoroughly cleaned, the sugar cookie may contain traces of peanut.

- When cooking oil is reused for different foods. An example would be French fries cooked in the same oil as cheese sticks. The oil may contain traces of cheese—a problem for people with a milk allergy.

- When utensils, pots and pans, or other kitchen equipment is used for multiple foods. An example would be using a spatula to pick up a brownie with walnuts and then reusing that same spatula to pick up a piece of cornbread. The cornbread then might contain traces of walnuts.

- When particles from one food enter another nearby through the movement of steam, splattering, or another method. An example would be boiling lobster next to a pot of soup. The splatter and/or steam from the lobster could get into the soup. As a result, the soup may contain traces of shellfish.[26]

Because cross contact can occur in a number of different ways, making choices about which foods are safe to eat requires careful research and communication, not only about a food's ingredients but also how it is prepared.

Much of our lives center around eating: We may grab a pizza with friends after a football game, enjoy ice cream and cake at a relative's birthday party, and snack on buttered popcorn and soda while at the movies. Besides being an enjoyable part of life, eating is essential to survival. So if eating food makes a person ill, that becomes a very big problem. Something as basic as eating can suddenly become a source of great anxiety.

Because food is such an integral part of our everyday lives, having food allergies can have an enormous impact on the food-allergic person—both emotionally and socially. Unlike everyone else, the food-allergic person can never be carefree when there is food involved.

Suddenly there is another question to ask for almost every conceivable decision. For example, is the baseball game a safe place, or do they offer peanuts that will be shelled by others while watching the game? Is the build-a-birdhouse workshop at the zoo safe, or will the birdseed contain nuts? If I go on the school's overnight camping trip, what will I eat and how will I stay safe? How will I tell my date that he cannot drink a milkshake and expect to kiss me goodnight?

Having to do this kind of thinking and questioning for every so-called normal activity can be both hard to accept and exhausting. For this reason, the food-allergic person can experience numerous emotions, including anxiety, fear, anger, and frustration. In fact, a recent study indicates that children who are allergic to peanuts have a higher level of anxiety than children with diabetes do.[1] The study concluded that due to the potentially life-threatening nature of their disease, children with peanut allergy are faced with more food and social restrictions than diabetic children.

The Emotional Impact

Growing up with a food allergy can be a difficult thing for young people. They may feel a broad range of emotions as they come to terms with the reality of their condition.

For example, some teens feel isolated or left out while others may feel angry or frustrated when they cannot participate in certain events or activities. Still others might feel so "different" or "weird" that it affects their self-esteem. And yet others accept the food allergy as part of life and learn to use it to their advantage.

"Young people have a number of things they're balancing. They're trying to figure out who they are, where they fit in, and yet they have a food allergy that they have to manage," explains

Anne Muñoz-Furlong, founder and CEO of the Food Allergy
and Anaphylaxis Network (FAAN).

> It's not a visible illness, and when we think about young kids
> socializing, it's all about food. That's what they do. They hang out,
> they eat pizza, they have parties, they go to the mall. They're always
> eating, munching, snacking. And when you have a food allergy,
> that puts a barrier in front of you and your friends. So the hardest
> part for them is trying to figure out how to fit in socially while
> managing their food allergy and not letting it get in the way, and
> that's not easy to do all the time.[2]

In general, Muñoz-Furlong says, the emotional impact of a
food allergy on a teen is greatly affected by how the family has
handled the allergy, how much they have incorporated it into
the child's everyday life, and how they have prepared the child.
If the parents have made it a part of life and not something that
the child should be embarrassed about, then it is more likely the
teen will share that view. However, if the parent pities the child,
or is embarrassed by the condition, then it is likely that the
child may feel sorry for himself or feel insecure about who he is.

According to Muñoz-Furlong:

> Some teenagers approach food allergies in a very matter-of-fact
> way. Their friends are aware of [the food allergy] and it's just one of
> the things that's part of the friend's character, like . . . eyeglasses or
> contact lenses. Other children are much more reserved, and
> private, and introspective, and those kids don't want to let anybody
> know [about the allergy], and they have a hard time sharing that
> information. . . . [This] then gets them into trouble because they
> are in situations where friends are suggesting, let's go eat in a place
> where this kid knows they shouldn't be, but they don't want to
> make a big deal of it and they think it will be a big deal to their
> friends. So they're constantly trying to balance how not to tell
> anybody, but how not to take such huge risks either.[3]

Impact on the Family

To say that families of allergic children experience abnormal
and excessive stress and anxieties is an understatement. Aside
from the worry about the child's safety, the parents may have

friends or other family members who do not believe the food allergy exists or believe that it is not as severe as described. As a result, they may try to give the child the restricted food to prove a point. When they succeed, they often cause a reaction.

One mother from New Zealand described the impact that food allergies have had on her family:

> Food-induced anaphylaxis is a terrible thing to live with. Life is described as living in a minefield—never knowing when one is going to step on a mine, or eat something that may contain the trace of food that will cause a fatal reaction. Living with . . . the total inability to be normal, be spontaneous or share social eating occasions with others is hugely stressful.[4]

"Food allergy is very much a family thing," explains Lisa Cipriano Collins, a marriage and family therapist who specializes in the emotional impact of managing food allergies. Collins also wrote the book *Caring for Your Child with Severe Food Allergies: Emotional Support and Practical Advice from a Parent Who's Been There*. She says:

> It's so hard to say it affects just one child, because siblings feel responsible and that can happen at a very young age, too. They understand they shouldn't expose their siblings to anything dangerous. They can be angry. The limits they feel are placed on them, too, places they can't go, or foods they can't have in the house, or the extra time spent with the food-allergic one. So they definitely feel like the food-allergic one has the spotlight in some ways.[5]

Additionally, siblings may become resentful or hurt by the extra attention the food-allergic kid receives. Or they may worry that the food-allergic brother or sister might die from the next reaction.

"A peanut allergy, like a bee sting allergic reaction, will cause my brother to have a reaction and then go into anaphylactic shock and possibly die," says sixteen-year-old Grant. "Any shape or form of peanut will cause a reaction. Also the smell triggers breathing problems such as asthma." He adds:

Daily life also presents problems for him and for us. Our family never deliberately encounters peanuts. We have to read labels on every food item at the store. We make restaurants search for any trace of peanuts when we eat there, for my brother's safety. It becomes a hassle on vacations, and also at football games because I must trade seats with my brother to get him away from the peanuts.[6]

"Food allergy is cruel," the mother from New Zealand says.

It offers no exceptions—no ability to relax and be normal, just for once. Just one bite can hurt—it can kill. Anyone who doesn't realize just how debilitating it is to live with food allergy simply has no idea. You can't know what it is like until you have had to live with it.

Despite the stresses, this mother says she is proud of the way in which her six-year-old boldly faces his food allergy:

He is amazing when he quietly watches the other kids in class sharing a birthday cake that another parent has brought into the class and knows that he can't have it. He quietly forgives his mother that I sometimes forget to have a safe alternative there for him to eat. He says "thanks but I can't eat that" to his teacher when she offers him a sweet for being good. . . . He is normal, though. He hates being different and he hates the fact that he has food allergies. Yes, I am proud of my six-year-old. But I wish with all my heart that he could just lead a happy and normal, uninhibited life.[7]

Impact on Teens

"In going through adolescence teens are experiencing a lot of growth in a lot of areas, trying to establish their identity, and what their friends think is really important," says Lisa Cipriano Collins, who has a teenage son with a peanut allergy. She says:

Some kids really don't like to feel different. Any time something's pointed out that there is something different about them, they don't like that. The EpiPen kind of sets them apart, or that they can't eat what everyone's eating, or they can't go where everyone's going. All of a sudden that's more troublesome than it was in grade school, or even middle school.

Young children often find it difficult to watch others eat foods to which they are allergic, as at birthday parties.

I think there's some fear there also, because as they get more independent and they want that independence, but all of a sudden they realize that they're in charge of it in certain situations and that's scary, I think. Adolescence is also a time of questioning what your parents have told you about everything and this is no exception. They might think that their parents have been too strict about it and then they want to try new things or do it differently. I also know a lot of kids who feel their parents are too lax and they don't really get it. Then all of a sudden they feel very fearful and develop some irrational fears.[8]

Moreover, adolescents and young adults are at the highest risk for dying from a food-induced allergic reaction—especially those with a peanut or tree nut allergy who also have asthma. In fact, in a study of thirty-two fatalities, 54 percent of those who died were between ten and nineteen years old.[9]

As young people become older, they increasingly spend more time away from home and with their friends. Consequently, they may do things that put them at risk, such as eating things they think are safe and going to restaurants that they should not go to. They also may not always carry an EpiPen everywhere they go, because they do not expect to have a reaction. Additionally, boys sometimes complain that it is difficult to conceal the EpiPen because it does not fit easily in their pockets.

However, Anne Muñoz-Furlong points out:

> Everybody says teenagers are risk takers and they sort of bring this on themselves. In none of the interviews that I have conducted when kids have died, and in none of the activities that I witnessed with my daughters when they made poor decisions, were the decisions based on risk taking. What I have come to understand is when we're talking about teenagers, they're not as cynical as we become as adults, so they don't see a risk.[10]

But perhaps the biggest threat to teens with food allergies is being in a group of friends who do not know the signs of a food-induced reaction. Or their friends do not know what to do to help them. Or, worse yet, their friends are not even aware that they have a food allergy.

In one case, a teenager lost consciousness while friends watched helplessly; none of them thought to call the rescue squad. At other times, food-allergic teens have been known to go off alone once a reaction begins because they do not want to call attention to themselves. Tragically, in several cases, friends have found food-allergic teens collapsed on the restroom floor clutching an asthma inhaler.[11]

Muñoz-Furlong explains:

> When we see kids that have died from their reactions, it always follows the same pattern and it's unfortunate. They go off by

themselves or something, or they're with a friend who does not know what to do. That's why our Be a Pal program was so important. It was created after several teenagers died and we realized in every single one of those cases that the child was with friends and, in a couple of cases, the friends just watched the individual collapse on the floor. They didn't know what to do. They didn't even know to call 911. So the Be a Pal program allows the friend to say, "Hey, I heard you have a peanut allergy. What's that about? What are the symptoms? What should I do if you have a reaction right now?" It opens up communication in a way that it's not driven only by the person with the allergy. And we believe that that method, to circle the kid with a group of friends that can keep them safe, is going to be the best way to go about this.[12]

Harassment

Further complicating the emotional aspects of food allergies, children and teens are sometimes teased and even bullied because of food allergies. A study reports that 50 percent of teens have been harassed about having allergies.[13]

For example, teens have been labeled as the kid who cannot eat eggs or called names like "peanut boy." Some feel ostracized if their schools do not allow food in classrooms because of them. And some teens have been threatened because of their food allergies. For example, a bully might use a peanut butter sand-wich as a weapon to get what he wants or smear egg on an egg-allergic person just to see what happens.

Joe, who is allergic to peanuts and tree nuts, says:

> For me, growing up with food allergies was a hard thing to deal with. Kids separated me, labeled me, and made fun of me because of my food allergies. They just did not realize how serious a problem it was—that one little bite could kill me.
>
> Elementary and middle school can seem to be the hardest thing to handle. . . . Every time you go to lunch, you have to ask the teacher if the food is okay. Other kids label you as Billy-the-kid-who-can't-have-pizza or Sally-the-girl-who-can't-eat-a-peanut-butter-and-jelly-sandwich. Kids will do cruel things like leave a

peanut in your lunch box or spit milk at you just to see what will happen.

In high school, people are a little bit older, more mature, and open-minded. Friends at lunch used to make sure that the food was okay and kept an eye on me. It was when I found my true group of friends that I found handling my allergies easier.[14]

The Social Impact

One of the most difficult aspects of living with a food allergy is the way in which it affects the person's social life—especially young people with food allergies.

By nature, teens are social creatures. They enjoy hanging out, going to parties, spending time at the mall, participating in school activities, dating, and so on.

As a result, food-allergic teens can feel left out when they have to pass up opportunities to be with their peers. Or, if they do decide to tag along but cannot eat anything, they may feel awkward watching everyone else eat and perhaps even a little jealous that they cannot be so carefree with something as simple as eating.

Children and teens are sometimes teased and even bullied because of food allergies. A study reports that 50 percent of teens have been harassed about having allergies.

Things that may be a nonissue to other teens present a major problem for the food-allergic teen. For example, a girl's parents may not let her go on a class trip to New York City because of her food allergy. Or a boy who wants to go on a white-water rafting trip wonders where he will put his EpiPen. All of this is just part of life for food-allergic people. They have to be on their toes at all times observing what is going on around them and making sure they are not putting their life at risk.

Many teens with food allergies have accepted these limitations. They realize that they must always be observant of

Teens with allergies have to be careful about things most people never have to consider—for instance, whether a date drinks a milkshake before a goodnight kiss.

what is going on around them. Yet most still try to live as normal a life as they can.

But even with the greatest resolve, having food allergies can still hurt. In fact, 94 percent of teens with food allergies feel that the hardest part of dealing with their allergy is the social isolation. Interestingly, for 50 percent of the parents, the hardest part is the fear of death.[15]

Restaurants

One of the most challenging social situations for food-allergic people is convincing the wait staff in a restaurant that their food allergies are a real medical condition and not a diet choice. This can be even harder for a teenager. But if they are not able to convince the wait staff, they may not get accurate information about ingredients and food preparation and could risk having a reaction. In almost all cases of an allergic reaction, the individual mistakenly believed that the food he or she was eating was safe. Moreover, 70 percent of deaths occur in connection with eating out at restaurants.[16]

Muñoz-Furlong says:

> Teens aren't taken seriously by wait staff and they don't know yet how to read a person and challenge them. If a waiter says, "It should be fine," . . . a teenager might say, "Okay, I don't want to rock the boat and make a big deal out of this." So these are some of the factors that get them into trouble and things that they struggle with. Then . . . not carrying medication, not recognizing symptoms, and then not knowing when to pull that fire alarm and say, "I'm in trouble." By the time that happens, it's usually too late.[17]

Some people use a "chef card" to relay important information to the restaurant's staff. This is a laminated card or business card listing the person's specific allergies. The card can be given to the restaurant manager for the chef to review. These cards demonstrate the seriousness of the person's allergy.

In a restaurant, people with food allergies typically have to order simply prepared items with a single ingredient, such as baked potatoes, steamed vegetables, and broiled meats. But they must still ask for help in selecting menu items and ask detailed questions about ingredients used and how the food is prepared. All of this can be intimidating for a young person.

Schools

Some kids with food allergies have no problem dealing with the various challenges that being in school every day brings. They are able to work around the obstacles their food allergies present and find safe and workable solutions. Perhaps it is because the staff members at their schools are more educated about and aware of food allergies and that makes it easier. Or perhaps they

Restaurants present special challenges to people with food allergies. For instance, lots of Asian food contains peanut, a common allergen.

are simply more resilient than some of their peers. Maybe their food allergies are only minor. For whatever reason, there are those with food allergies who sail through school without a problem.

But for other young people with food allergies, attending school every day is not always easy. They experience all types of emotions with regard to school.

For example, a middle school student might have panic attacks in the school lunchroom while a first grader might cry when he has to get on the bus. Or a high school student is so afraid of what a date would say about not being able to eat peanuts while out with her that she withdraws socially.

In fact, Lisa Cipriano Collins says that the far-reaching and intense emotional responses to the daily challenges of food allergies can run the gamut from mild to severe and can become an issue at various times throughout the food-allergic person's life.[18]

Further complicating that matter are the regular challenges and sometimes hazards a food-allergic person must face while attending school. In fact, food allergies are a growing health and safety concern in the classroom, according to a study, the *Impact of Food Allergies on School Nursing Practice.*

The study found that 44 percent of the school nurses reported an increase in elementary-age students with food allergies in the classroom over the last five years. And more than one third of the nurses said they had ten or more students in school with food allergies.[19] Finally, 87 percent stated that, compared with other health-related issues, food allergies among school-age children is somewhat or very serious.[20]

"Protecting a child with food allergies requires cooperation of the staff and proper educational tools, especially in a classroom setting," says Muñoz-Furlong. "The Department of Education and state governments across the country must provide standardized training programs to school staff to address this growing health and safety issue."[21]

Moreover, food allergies in schools have become a hot topic. Sometimes parents of severely food-allergic children clash not only with school officials but also with other parents. Out of fear that their child will have a fatal reaction, the parents may try to demand that the allergen, most commonly peanuts, be completely banned from the school.

Obviously, parents of children without food allergies sometimes find this demand unreasonable and may be even more upset if their child is a picky eater and will only eat peanut butter sandwiches. They are then faced with the problem of what to feed their child and begin to make demands of their own. School officials then are caught in the middle trying to meet the needs of those children with food allergies and those children without food allergies.

Under federal law, children with food allergies cannot be excluded from school functions because of their food allergies. Additionally, allergen-free substitutions are required for children participating in the free breakfast or lunch program. This must be provided at no cost to the family, provided the child has written documentation from the physician about the child's food allergies.[22]

Overall, if schools have a plan for dealing with food-allergic children, including educating all the staff about the risks and how to administer treatment, the students at risk are more likely to experience fewer symptoms and fewer medical emergencies. When schools meet the needs of food-allergic students, the students can function to their maximum potential, including having better attendance records and being more alert during class. And they are less likely to be restricted from physical activities and extra events like field trips, making their overall school experience a positive one.[23]

Travel

"Bon voyage!" To most people, this expression of goodwill brings a feeling of excitement as they leave for a much-needed vacation or travel to another city to take in the sights and visit with friends. But for the severely food-allergic, it may also be combined with a slight twinge of anxiety as they run through a mental checklist of all the things they need to do to prepare for the trip.

"Do I have my medications? Did I pack the letter from my allergist confirming my allergies? Do I have enough 'safe' food packed? Did I remember handy-wipes for quick cleaning? Where did I put the list of hospitals and allergists' phone numbers? What did I do with the list of restaurants that are safe? . . . "

When it comes to planning a trip—whether it is a one-day road trip or a one-week vacation, the amount of planning, packing, and consideration it takes is almost unbelievable to the non-food-allergic. "Is it really necessary?" they may ask. The answer is almost always "yes" because the food-allergic person's life depends on being prepared.

The good news for food-allergic people is there are now more options than ever. Lots of food-allergic people have traveled all around the world without a problem. But travel away from home where a certain comfort level has been established is never without challenges. Perhaps one of the biggest obstacles for the food-allergic person is flying in an airplane—especially for individuals with peanut and tree nut allergies, which are more likely than other allergies to be life threatening.

To date, there are still some airlines that do not make any accommodations for passengers with peanut and tree nut allergies, including Continental, ATA, and America West. However, as of January 2003, United, US Airways, American, Northwest, and the Delta Shuttle were the domestic airlines that do not serve peanut snacks. American and some other airlines serve some tree nut mixtures. Aer Lingus and British Air are two international carriers that do not serve peanut snacks.[24]

Even with such restrictions, no airline can guarantee a peanut-free flight. Their in-flight meals may contain peanuts or tree nuts, or other passengers may carry on peanut products. Occasionally, an airline will agree to offer only peanut-free and nut-free snacks, like pretzels, during a flight if someone notifies the airline of his or her allergy well in advance. And, if asked, airlines will sometimes make an announcement and ask passengers not to consume peanut or tree nut products during the flight.

At other times, the airlines can be extremely difficult to work with. Michelle Risinger says:

> Every time that we called ahead to double check if nuts would or would not be served on a flight, whatever we were told was always the exact opposite of what happened. . . . I've been kicked off planes before. I had a pilot standing in front of me one time telling me in front of the entire cabin that the plane was going to take off because these people had paid for their nuts, and if I wanted to get off, I could. So I've just had really bad experiences with flying.[25]

Two other things that must be considered by the food-allergic person traveling by airplane are the new rules for baggage screening and the new rules regarding carry-on items—specifically medications.

In 2002, the Transportation Security Administration (TSA) issued an updated list of items that airline passengers can bring on board. This list included syringes containing medication as long as it has a professional label with the medication or manufacturer's name. (This statement should include the EpiPen.) The Food Allergy and Anaphylaxis Network advises its members to carry additional documentation, including a doctor's note and the prescription label from the pharmacy.[26]

As for baggage screening, the TSA has implemented new rules that may present a challenge for allergic people traveling with food. According to the FAAN:

> All baggage will now be screened and the TSA Web site . . . suggests that travelers "avoid packing food and drink items in checked baggage." Food is not on the forbidden list, but may bring extra attention during the security check, thereby taking additional time at the airport.[27]

The TSA says that passengers are permitted to bring food onto airplanes in their carry-on bags, but it must go through the X-ray machine at the security checkpoint before boarding.[28]

When traveling abroad, people with food allergies need to take extra precautions as well. They need to make sure they are understood when eating in foreign restaurants, determine where medical help can be found, and be sure they have proper health insurance coverage. Before going abroad, they should also check with the foreign embassy of the country they will be visiting to make sure their medications are not considered illegal narcotics.

Dealing With Public Perception

Convincing others of the seriousness of food allergies can be difficult at times. In fact, it can be both stressful and frustrating when other people do not take the condition seriously. This lack of understanding can raise the level of fear and anxiety the food-allergic person experiences. Because if the people he is trying to communicate with do not believe the seriousness of his condition, he may not take the steps needed to help himself stay safe.

To people who do not have food allergies and who are not familiar with food allergies, the precautions a food-allergic person must take may seem like ludicrous steps taken by over-cautious hypochondriacs. Additionally, some people will even go so far as to try to "trick" the person into eating what he or she is allergic to in order to prove a point. Although these

When Kissing Can Kill

Because food does not have to be eaten to cause an allergic reaction, every form of contact with food has to be considered when trying to avoid an allergic reaction—even kissing. For example, if a teenage girl is allergic to peanuts and her boyfriend eats anything containing peanuts and then kisses her, she could have an allergic reaction.

Tragically, recent news bears this out: In November 2005, Christina Desforges died after kissing her boyfriend, who had eaten a snack containing peanut butter. The fifteen-year-old girl, who lived near Quebec, was treated with adrenaline for anaphylactic shock but did not recover. Desforges' friends said that neither they nor her boyfriend knew of the allergy.[29]

Researchers at the University of California reported that 5.3 percent of the food-allergic people they surveyed had experienced reactions after being kissed on the neck, face, lips, or cheek. Within one minute of the kiss, they began itching, swelling, and developing hives where they were kissed. Additionally, some reacted even after their partners had brushed their teeth.[30]

Therefore, it is extremely important that people with food allergies avoid kissing someone who has eaten the food to which they are allergic.

According to Anne Muñoz-Furlong, founder and CEO of FAAN:

> When you've got, say, a peanut allergy or a nut allergy, and you're going to be kissing somebody and they've just had peanut butter, that could put you at risk. So it's a very tall order to get a teenager who's trying to get used to their own emotional feelings for another person and wanting to be close to that person, giving them the courage and finding the words to say, "But I have an allergy. If you've just eaten peanuts or walnuts, you can't kiss me." That's not easy to do probably for most adults. It certainly is real difficult for teenagers.[31]

beliefs are by no means accurate (most food-allergic people would love to be able to eat whatever they want), they can be very hurtful. A true food allergy is a medically documented disease that should be taken very seriously by everyone.

"There's a little bit greater public awareness than there was, but there's still some ignorance and some misconceptions,"

People who do not have food allergies often do not understand how serious they are. They may not know that sharing food, like this couple is doing, can be life threatening to a food-allergic person.

explains Lisa Cipriano Collins. "People think, 'Oh, they can have a little,' or [it will just make them] sneeze and cough or something. You can't really trust that people know, down to the seventeen-year-old waitress that's supposed to be helping you stay safe."[32]

For food-allergic individuals, being constantly cautious and aware is a fact of life. They know they must take the steps needed to protect themselves even if they seem annoying or appear crazy. If they do not act responsibly, an accident could happen, and it could even cost them their life. So, for most food-allergic people, being looked at like they are fanatical sometimes is worth the price of staying safe.

Legal Concerns

The legal picture of food allergies is a changing one, and it will continue to be that way as new lawsuits are brought forth and decided. Currently, the most frequent legal challenge for parents of food-allergic children are the requests to sign legal waivers about administering epinephrine. These waivers indicate that the food-allergic person is giving up the right to ever take legal action. Most experts consider them a bad idea. For example, the American Academy of Allergy, Asthma and Immunology states:

> Parents should be advised never to sign a liability waiver absolving the school of responsibility for administering epinephrine. Epinephrine is the first drug that should be used in the emergency management of a child having a potentially life-threatening allergic reaction.[33]

Sometimes, though, school staff show an unwillingness to care for food-allergic children. In addition, they may refuse to take responsibility for administering the EpiPen. In the eyes of the law, however, this type of action may be considered discrimination. And worse yet, it is life threatening for the food-allergic person.

Whether or not food allergies are a disability covered under Section 504 of the Rehabilitation Act of 1973 and the Individuals with Disabilities Education Act (IDEA) is another area of debate.

Section 504 is a civil rights law designed to prohibit discrimination on the basis of disability. The law applies to a program or institution that receives federal funds so that the students with handicaps or disabilities receive a free and appropriate public education. Under this law, a food allergy may be considered a disability.

Essentially, a 504 Plan is a written agreement between the parents and the school. The plan outlines the steps the school will take to make sure that the student is kept safe and allowed access to all activities during the school day. Because many schools already have taken steps to manage students with food allergies, a 504 Plan is not always necessary.

Another act of interest to food-allergic kids and their parents is the IDEA. This act requires public schools to make available "a free appropriate public education in the least restrictive environment" to all eligible children with disabilities.

As a result, public school systems are required to develop appropriate Individualized Education Programs (IEPs) for each child. The specific special education and related services outlined in each IEP reflect the individualized needs of each student. Although IEPs vary from person to person, one element of a food-allergic child's plan might require an allergen-free table in the cafeteria. Another might be a program to train school personnel to recognize and treat a reaction. Other elements might address class trips, art projects, and classroom parties that involve food.

There have also been a handful of lawsuits regarding discrimination (or violating a food-allergic person's rights.) One example is a settlement agreement in 2003 between the U.S. Department of Justice and a private military high school for boys. This settlement was reached after the school denied enrollment to a student with food allergies. As a result, the school will establish policies that address the successful management of students with life-threatening food allergies.

Although the settlement applies only to the school involved, it appears that the U.S. government takes food allergies seriously. As a result, discrimination against students with food allergies will not be allowed—even in private schools.[34] In fact, according to the U.S. Department of Justice, Title III of the Americans with Disabilities Act (ADA) applies even to private schools. In other words, private schools are not allowed to refuse a qualified person with a disability to participate in its program. Additionally, if the private school receives federal funding, they also must abide by Section 504 and IDEA.[35]

The Positive Side of Living With Food Allergies

Despite the challenges that come with severe food allergies, there are also some positive aspects.

According to Lisa Cipriano Collins:

> Children who cope successfully with food allergies from an early age often have a level of maturity and sensitivity far beyond their chronological age. Because of the self-discipline required in addition to the normal challenges of growing up, food-allergic children often become stronger, more self-assured people. The ongoing need for communication between themselves and others contributes to their ability to relate well to other people. The need to communicate among family members can provide a satisfying sense of cohesion and belonging.
>
> Food-allergic children also need to identify and cultivate "real" friends. By learning to look for in others . . . qualities like cooperation, accommodation, and compassion, food-allergic children in turn have these same qualities to offer.[36]

Tina, who is allergic to peanuts, tree nuts, sesame seeds, and poppy seeds, tells how her experiences have made her stronger:

> Ever since I was an infant, I have had terrible food allergies. . . . By the time I reached middle school, I was tall, spindly and able to name about every hospital in New England.
>
> Knowing that accidental ingestion of certain foods could kill me, I was forced to grow up and take complete responsibility for myself. At eleven years old, I was mature enough to make life-or-death decisions.
>
> As time went on, my allergies seemed only to get worse. . . . For six years, half of my public education, I was not able to eat in any school cafeteria. Being isolated each afternoon while others ate lunch and being ostracized by classmates because they weren't allowed to bring food into classrooms were difficult burdens.
>
> It did not take long for me to realize, however, that my food allergies did not have to define me. I worked hard in school and excelled in extracurricular activities to counter this void in my life. Having food allergies helped me realize one of my strongest personality traits: the strength to overcome adversity. Even though

It is important for people with food allergies to have friends who will support them and who know what to do if a reaction occurs.

nature seemed to be against me, I conquered my allergies by living the most normal life that I could.[37]

In fact, living as normal a life as possible seems to be the goal of almost every food-allergic individual. They quickly learn that their food allergies do not have to define them and that there is so much more to life than food. The focus for the food-allergic person becomes more about activities and events rather than restaurants and desserts.

What Science Is Doing

Food allergies were first documented in the fourth century B.C. by Hippocrates, a Greek physician, who is often called the father of medicine. He noted that milk could cause hives and stomach upset.

Although food allergies are not a new phenomenon, until recently there has been very little accurate information available. One extreme example occurred in 1997 when an allergist told the mother of a six-month-old baby who was allergic to cow's milk that there was nothing that could be done for her baby's food allergies.

"Your daughter is allergic to the protein in milk," the doctor told her. "She'll die before she is one year old. I suggest you go home, love her and prepare yourself. . . . There is nothing I can do. There is nothing that can be done with food allergies."[1]

But this mother refused to give up. When she found a dairy-free cookbook, she knew there was hope. She immediately made some phone calls and spoke with one of the top doctors in the field—Hugh Sampson. Dr. Sampson assured the mother that her baby would not die and that there were in fact many children like her that lived full lives.

Great strides have been made in food allergy education, diagnosis, treatment, and research. At the forefront are two very important organizations—the Food Allergy Initiative (FAI) and the Food Allergy and Anaphylaxis Network (FAAN).

FAI is a nonprofit organization that raises funds to invest in food allergy research designed to find a cure and improve treatment options. The organization also strives to raise public awareness about the seriousness of food allergies.

FAAN, which was founded in 1991, is the world's largest nonprofit organization providing information about food allergy. The goals of the organization include raising public awareness, providing advocacy and education, and advancing research on behalf of those affected by food allergy and anaphylaxis. Anne Muñoz-Furlong started the organization because very little food allergy information was available at the time and her own daughter had been diagnosed with a milk and egg allergy as an infant. Muñoz-Furlong says:

> Twenty years ago nobody believed babies could have allergies. They didn't really believe in food allergies at all, and nobody wanted to test her to see if that's what she had. So there was—and there still is—a misconception that you have to wait until a child is three years old until you skin test them. So we were up against trying to convince the medical side that there's something wrong with this child. She's growing and she's fine, but every time she eats she has projectile vomiting, hives, all the classic symptoms of what we now

know are allergies. Once we got her diagnosed, we were basically on our own. The doctor said, "Go home and avoid milk and eggs," and that was the extent of the patient education that was given to us.

I learned by trial and error, at her expense, that there were synonyms for things like milk and eggs. And that experience impacted myself and our family so much that I wanted to do something that would help other families not have to go through what we had gone through. So that was where the idea for FAAN got started—to create a clearinghouse of basic, but practical, information that parents could count on that was science based, so that they could learn everything they need to know about managing a child's food allergies.[2]

As a result, FAAN has done just that. Additionally, the organization has sponsored research programs and has been instrumental in encouraging other entities to research food allergies. For example, in 2005, the National Institutes of Health committed $5 million for food allergy research. And FAAN hopes for more in the future.

To date, there are two major areas of food allergy research: studying the causes of food allergies and searching for a cure. Recently, there have been some major breakthroughs in food allergy research. The findings may bring hope to the millions suffering from the condition.[3]

Studying the Causes

To prevent further development of food allergies, scientists around the world are studying the causes. One popular area of study is the role genetics plays in the development of food allergies. While scientists believe genetics plays a part in the creation of food allergies, they do not really understand how this happens. Additionally, no major genes have been identified that cause food allergy.[4]

Still, a number of researchers are concentrating on a person's genetic background. They hope to determine what role an individual's genetic makeup has in influencing the development of food allergies.

One example is a recent study of peanut allergy among twins. Researchers performed the study to determine if genetic factors influence peanut allergy. Studies of twins are often used to provide information about the genetic factors of a disease.

The study included fifty-eight pairs of twins, fourteen identical and forty-four fraternal. At least one person from each pair—seventy of the individuals in the study—had a history of peanut allergy. What the researchers discovered was that in 64 percent of the identical twin pairs, both twins were allergic to peanuts. However, in the fraternal twin pairs, only 7 percent of the twins shared a peanut allergy.

By using this information in combination with already established models, the researchers were able to calculate an 82 to 87 percent chance of inheriting a peanut allergy. When genetic factors were not considered, the chances of getting a peanut allergy dropped to 19 percent. Although additional research must be done to determine the exact role of genetics in food allergies, it is clear that it does play a role.[5]

Scientists believe genetics plays a part in the creation of food allergies, but they do not really understand how this happens. No major genes have been identified that cause food allergy.

Another area of study is the role a child's mother plays in the development of food allergies. A child's mother not only contributes 50 percent of her genes to her baby, but also her body provides the exclusive environment for the baby during the nine months of pregnancy. And she continues to be a major factor if she is breast-feeding the baby.

With this in mind, several studies have been conducted, including one in Norway, one in Germany, and one in the United States, to determine how the mother may contribute to

Researchers are looking into the genetic basis for allergies. Studies have shown that identical twins have a strong likelihood of sharing an allergy, while fraternal twins are no more likely than ordinary siblings to do so.

the development of her child's food allergies. The Norwegian and German studies showed a connection between cesarean birth and the development of food allergies. The reasons, however, are still unknown.

Additionally, the American study demonstrated the connection between a mother's age and the development of food allergies. In fact, food-allergic children are three times more likely to have a mother who was over thirty years old at the time of birth than nonallergic children.[6]

In another study, a group of researchers watched two strains of mice. Both strains had been sensitized to cow's milk and peanut. They found that only one strain had developed antibodies to cow's milk and had symptoms of an allergic reaction. In addition, both strains developed IgE antibodies to peanut, but only one mouse strain had allergic reactions to peanut. Interestingly, it was the same mouse strain that reacted to milk.[7]

Next, the scientists will try to find out why one strain reacted and the other one did not. Ultimately, research like this should help scientists begin to understand why some children react to foods while others do not.

In a third study, conducted by an Austrian group, scientists fed fish allergens to two groups of mice. In addition to the fish, one of the groups also received antacids while the other group did not. They found that the mice that received the antacids developed IgE antibodies to the fish and the other group did not.

None of the mice developed antibodies to food they ate regularly, but only to new foods. What the investigators concluded was that when antacid medication was given to the mice, it affected digestion and the acid level in the stomach. Ultimately, this left food proteins more intact and led to the creation of a food allergy.

Although more research needs to be done, this study raises the question of whether or not antacids, which frequently are used to treat acid reflux in infants, could actually be causing some food allergies in the long run.[8]

Searching for a Cure

Scientists around the world are trying to unravel the food allergy mystery. They hope to put the pieces of the puzzle together someday. For example, some scientists are studying specific food allergens to determine which proteins in foods are causing the reactions. This information is needed to understand how foods are structured. Once the structure of foods is better understood, scientists can use this information to develop remedies that could reduce and even eliminate the allergenic properties of these foods.

Other scientists are working on a potential vaccine to prevent food allergy from developing in high-risk children. According to researchers of one study, they are getting closer to developing a peanut vaccine. During a 2003 study, peanut-allergic mice received a vaccine. The vaccine was made with slightly altered (genetically engineered) peanut proteins and *E. coli* bacteria. The proteins were altered so that they would not cause an allergic reaction, and the *E. coli* was killed and given to the peanut-allergic mice.[9]

Dr. Hugh Sampson, professor of pediatrics and immunology at Mount Sinai School of Medicine in New York, says:

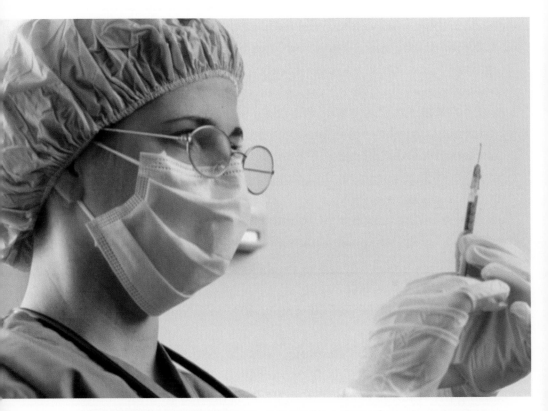

Researchers hope to develop a vaccine for peanut allergy. Progress is being made, but a vaccine is many years away.

We've identified the genes in the peanut plant that make these proteins, we've altered those genes in such a way that this protein will no longer cause an allergic reaction when we give it to somebody, but it will turn off that patient's allergic response to peanut.[10]

After getting the vaccine, the mice were later fed peanut. The scientists found that the mice had reduced reactions or no reactions to the peanut.

"This particular vaccine, which could be adapted for human use, provides some hope that we may be able to treat peanut allergy in human patients and that we will no longer see symptoms," says Sampson. Additionally, Sampson indicated that the vaccine would still need to be tested on humans before it becomes available.[11]

"I would say within the next five to ten years we're going to see more of these animal studies moving into human trials," adds Muñoz-Furlong, "but then it's a long process once those get started before you see something in the supermarket or in the drugstore."[12]

Other researchers are studying therapies that will reduce IgE levels. Lower levels would mean that people would no longer react after ingesting a particular food. One example of this is anti-IgE therapy.

The purpose of the anti-IgE therapy study is to determine whether or not drugs like Xolair can effectively and safely reduce the symptoms of an allergic reaction in peanut-allergic people. Xolair is a prescription medication already on the market for treatment of severe allergic asthma.

During the initial study, researchers found that a similar drug "collected" and "bound" the peanut antibody in the body. In addition, all patients taking the drug showed a decrease in the IgE levels at the end of the study, and most were able to tolerate larger amounts of peanut before having an allergic reaction.

Xolair also works by binding IgE and preventing the release of chemicals and histamines from cells, which can cause the symptoms of an allergic reaction. The study will also compare how much peanut Xolair-treated patients can tolerate.[13]

"This important study in peanut allergy highlights the promise of anti-IgE research and therapies across a range of allergic conditions," says Tanox CEO Nancy Chang. Tanox is currently developing Xolair in collaboration with Novartis Pharma AG and Genetech, Inc. Chang says that her company is looking forward to further study of anti-IgE therapy in food allergies and other diseases.[14]

Muñoz-Furlong adds:

> [They hope to find] a treatment to regulate some of these severe reactions so that you have more of a tolerance for when you make a mistake and it doesn't cost you your life. You will still get sick, but you're not having a life-threatening reaction. The reality is we're probably looking at five to ten years before we have something on the market for mass distribution, simply because these studies go so slowly.[15]

Everyone affected by food allergies hopes that one day there will be a cure for this life-altering and sometimes life-threatening condition. They also hope for a better understanding of the cause and improved treatment options.

But for now, there is no cure for food allergies. Once someone has food allergies, there are no medicines to make it go away. The only way people can make sure they do not have a reaction is to never taste, touch, or even smell the food.

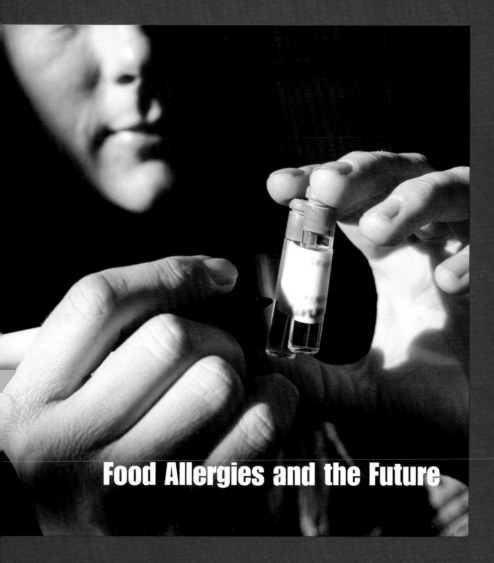

Food Allergies and the Future

Food allergies are one of life's major health challenges. For the food-allergic person, every bite of food must be questioned and analyzed to be sure that it is safe to eat. And this must be done each time the person eats, whether it is a snack or a meal, and no matter where it will take place—at home, at a friend's house, at school, or at a restaurant. It is the only way to prevent an allergic reaction, because just one taste of the wrong food can be lethal.

But the future for people with food allergies does hold promise. Research efforts have improved the knowledge base of scientists around the world, while educational efforts have improved awareness and understanding. What has been accomplished so far, though, is just the beginning. There is still a lot of work to do. For example, in the past five years, peanut allergies in children have doubled. And the estimated number of Americans with food allergies has climbed from 6 million to approximately 11 million, and no one knows why for sure.

Despite the increase in food allergies and the seriousness of the issue, too few people truly understand food allergies or take them seriously. There are cases where a relative, a friend, or a teacher does not believe that a food allergy is as serious as it is. Instead, they wrongly believe that "just a taste" will not hurt. Or they assume that the food-allergic person is paranoid or exaggerating the problem. But worse yet is when the food-allergic person does not take his or her allergy seriously.

For this reason, educating both the people affected by food allergies and the general public is still one of the most important parts of food allergy management. With a better understanding of food allergies comes improved legislation to help protect food-allergic individuals.

Education and Legislation

"Until there is a cure, education is the key"—this is the slogan of FAAN and perhaps the single most important aspect of caring for food allergies. Not only do patients and their families need to be well educated about the dangers of food allergies and the importance of strict avoidance, but the general public also needs to be educated. Institutions such as schools, restaurants, and airlines need to adopt policies that will make life for the food-allergic person both safer and easier.

Anne Muñoz-Furlong says:

> My personal goal is to [get] food allergy to the point where people respect it as much as when you announce that you have diabetes, high blood pressure, or heart disease. [If you have one of those conditions,] no one tries to convince you that you're crazy, that it

doesn't exist, "Just eat another steak and you might feel better." My mission is to make sure that people understand this is a medical condition. Don't second-guess people, try to bribe them, hide things to prove to them they're making it up, because you're playing with people's lives.

Overall, Muñoz-Furlong says she is encouraged by what the future may hold for food allergies. "I think we are going to continue to see an increase in awareness and understanding and, with that, will come policy changes that are much needed for schools, restaurants, the food industry and so forth."[1]

Changes in Restaurants

Although food allergy policies in restaurants have been slow to come, there are indications that the educational efforts of organizations like FAAN are having an effect. For example, in 2002, the National Restaurant Association (NRA) took its first step toward improving food allergy awareness and training among the industry's 11.6 million employees.[2]

"A lot of customers have a lot of different requests. It could be a diet; it could be allergies. The one you take most seriously as a chef is allergies," says Marcus Samuelsson, chef and co-owner of Aquavit restaurant in New York City.[3]

The NRA, with assistance from FAAN, created the Food Allergy Training Program for Restaurants and Food Services. The program includes a video and a manual that provides important information on food allergies. It also offers ideas on how to handle food-allergic customers from the moment they look at the menu until the time they place their order and ultimately get their food. There is also a section on what to do in an emergency.

According to Steven C. Anderson, the association's president and chief executive officer:

The National Restaurant Association and the restaurant industry prides itself on having a well-informed, trained and educated staff

Hollywood Looks at Food Allergies

As awareness about food allergies increases, there has also been an increase in the number of times the condition is mentioned in the popular media. In fact, in 2005, there were two movies that had characters with food allergies and two TV programs. However, in all but one of the cases, the portrayal of food allergies was not completely accurate, nor was it sensitive to those affected by food allergies.

Perhaps the worst offender was the movie *Monster-In-Law*, which ironically debuted during Food Allergy Awareness Week. In the movie, the character Viola Fields (Jane Fonda) wants to ruin her son's marriage to Charlie (Jennifer Lopez), who has a serious nut allergy. In one scene, Fields tries to get rid of her unwanted daughter-in-law for good by putting crushed nuts in a gravy boat.

According to FAAN, the movie not only makes fun of food allergies, but also sets the stage for a "copycat" to do the same thing in real life.

"Better examples need to be set," says Anne Muñoz-Furlong. "I doubt New Line Cinema would permit a scene where a diabetic would be given an overdose of insulin. We are seeing more Hollywood movies and shows portraying food allergies in an unsafe and very uneducated light."[4]

Additionally, the movie *Hitch* and an episode of *The Simpsons* each made fun of an individual with food allergies. In *Hitch*, Alex Hitchens, known as "Hitch" (Will Smith), has an allergic reaction to seafood. In the movie, his throat becomes scratchy, his eyes get puffy, his breathing is labored, and he

(continued on next page)

on all aspects of food safety including allergy safety, in restaurants nationwide. . . . If a patron informs the staff that he/she has particular food allergies, the server and chef will ensure that the customer is accommodated and provided customized menu options to meet their health needs.[5]

Although examples of food-allergic patrons being accommodated are not widespread at the moment, there are signs that the industry may be moving in that direction. For example, some restaurants have started indicating on their breaks out in hives. When another person identifies his reaction as a food allergy, he responds like many Americans, says FAAN, and does not take it seriously. Later Hitch races to the pharmacy for Benadryl when he actually may need epinephrine.

"We hope not only does Hitch 'get the girl' but he also needs to go see an allergist," says Muñoz-Furlong. "[His allergic reaction] can be funny to watch in a movie, but if you are ever with someone experiencing a food allergic reaction it can be quite frightening."[6]

On the positive side, in April 2005 PBS debuted an episode of *Arthur* called "Binky Goes Nuts: Understanding Peanut Allergies." In the episode, which has a companion educational guide designed for school nurses and educators of children ages four to eight, Binky has many questions about his peanut allergy. He wants to know if he will be forced to live without Chinese food, if he will be able to eat with his friends, and if his mom will ever calm down. Ultimately, Binky learns that the only way he can keep from "going nuts" is by learning everything he can about his food allergy.

"Over the years, I have received many requests from kids and adults asking us to tackle the subject of peanut allergies in an *Arthur* episode," says Marc Brown, the creator of *Arthur* and series executive creative producer. "Given that so many of our young fans and their parents deal with food allergies every day, we have a unique opportunity to make a real difference."[7]

menus when a particular dish contains peanuts or tree nuts—two very potent food allergies.

Additionally, some large organizations like Walt Disney World have developed policies specifically for people with food allergies. According to their policy, all the table service restaurants at Disney that accept "priority seating" can accommodate people with allergies to peanuts, tree nuts, fish, shellfish, milk, eggs, soy, and wheat. The requirement is that the food must be ordered seventy-two hours in advance.[8]

Some of the restaurants aboard Disney's Cruise Lines will also accommodate food-allergic passengers. People need to alert the cruise line about their allergies when making reservations.

In addition to the NRA's training program, there has been recent legislation in a number of states designed to improve the way in which restaurants meet the needs of food-allergic people. For example, New Jersey passed a law in January 2005 that calls for the creation of a public information campaign called "Ask Before You Eat." This campaign is designed to inform the public about food allergies and anaphylaxis. The law also requires restaurant managers to inform their employees about allergenic ingredients in the food prepared at the restaurant.[9]

Similar bills were introduced in Illinois, Massachusetts, Connecticut, and Rhode Island between 2003 and 2004. Although none were signed into law, it is apparent that state legislators are aware of the food allergy issue and the challenges found in restaurants. The bills also show that the national environment is likely to improve over the next few years.[10]

Changes in Schools

There are roughly 3 million school-aged children who have food allergies, and this number is climbing.[11] For this reason, improving the ability of the nation's schools to handle food allergies will become even more important in the future.

Studies also identify a number of reasons why schools are of particular concern for food-allergic children and their families. One study of thirteen fatal and near-fatal anaphylactic reactions showed that four of the six children who died experienced the fatal reactions at school. However, none of the near-fatal reactions did. Together, these facts call into question the ability of schools to deal with such medical emergencies.[12]

Another study showed that many reactions from peanuts and tree nuts were caused by food in class projects.[13] Another

A typical school lunch. Schools' abilities to plan for and deal with food allergies will become even more important in the future.

study of food-allergic children showed that 44 percent of the children had accidental ingestions in two years.[14]

In June 2004, the American Medical Association (AMA) recommended that schools do more to educate both students and teachers about food allergies. The AMA also recommended that schools have guidelines for managing food allergy emergencies and that they make sure that EpiPens are available and staff are trained to use them.[15]

"School staff need to be trained to prevent and respond to food-allergy reactions," says Dr. J. Edward Hill, Jr., of the AMA. "Education, training and emergency preparedness will keep children with food allergies safe at school."[16]

In addition to not being well educated with regard to food allergies, many schools also have strict policies against carrying medication while at school. Instead, medicines—including the lifesaving drug epinephrine—are locked in the nurse's office or kept at the front office. For severely food-allergic children, this policy could put their lives at risk when every second counts during a reaction.

Some states are starting to recognize this issue. In September 2004, California Governor Arnold Schwarzenegger signed a bill permitting thousands of students to carry and administer epinephrine in school.[17] California became the sixth state to adopt such a law, joining Delaware, New Hampshire, Michigan, Minnesota, and Maine.

Overall, safeguarding a child against a food-allergic reaction at school takes the cooperation and understanding of all the parents, doctors, school administrators, teachers, school nurses, food service staff, and students.

"What I am looking forward to in schools is that every school has a plan in place before the children arrive for how they handle a food allergy, and that they work with the parents to customize the plan for that child," says Anne Muñoz-Furlong.[18]

At the college level, there are signs of improvement as well. For example, at Harvard University roughly 8 percent of the student population has food allergies or food sensitivities.[19] To accommodate its students, the executive chef for dining services will work directly with any student who has special dietary needs.

Improved Food Labels

Reading food labels is one of the most important parts of avoiding food allergens. For years, though, this was not as easy as it sounds. Instead of simple terms like "milk" and "eggs" listed on the labels, manufacturers often would use scientific terms like casein (milk) and albumin (eggs). But that is all about to change.

In August 2004, President George W. Bush signed a new food-labeling bill. This legislation, called the Food Allergen and Consumer Protection Act (FALCPA), will take effect January 1, 2006. Then, food manufacturers must list in plain language the presence of any of the eight major food allergens (milk, egg, peanut, tree nut, fish, shellfish, wheat, and soy). They must also state if the eight food allergens are used in spices, flavorings, additives, or colorings, which had been exempt from allergen labeling before. This requirement closes a loophole that puts people at risk from unlisted ingredients.[20]

Muñoz-Furlong states:

> This is an historic piece of legislation for the millions of Americans with food allergies. After 13 years of working collaboratively with the food industry, medical community and members of Congress, we are assured what is on the label is in the package. The legislation takes the guesswork out of all the different scientific references for simple names like milk and egg.[21]

In the past five years, peanut allergies in children have doubled, and the estimated number of Americans with food allergies has climbed from 6 million to approximately 11 million. No one knows why for sure.

Improved labels have made it easier for people with allergies to tell whether or not a food contains dangerous allergens. But it is important to check the label every time.

FALCPA also calls on the federal government to:

- make improvements in the way food-allergy data is collected

- keep abreast of food allergy research

- report to Congress on inspections of food manufacturing facilities and the ways in which these facilities can reduce or eliminate cross contact

- consider revising the Food Code to provide allergen-free preparation guidelines for food service establishments

- investigate consumer preferences regarding precautionary statements on food labels.[22]

The last point refers to food manufacturers' practice of putting statements of food labels such as "May contain traces of peanut." Some experts believe that manufacturers may use these statements to reduce their liability. In addition, consumers with food allergies sometimes find these statements limiting and frustrating. In most cases, they would prefer to know simply "Yes, this product contains peanuts."[23]

Genetically Modified Allergen-Free Food

One area of study that shows future promise, although somewhat controversial, is genetically modified foods. These foods are also known as GM foods, GE (genetically engineered) foods, or GMOs (genetically modified organisms). They have been changed to produce desirable qualities, such as crops that are resistant to pests or foods that are less allergenic.

Researchers at Tulane University in New Orleans are looking at the possibility of genetically modifying shrimp to remove the proteins that cause allergic reactions. They believe this may be possible because the major shrimp protein that causes allergies has been identified. In addition, there is a better understanding of what occurs during a reaction. Research on soy and peanuts is contributing to the shrimp study.[24]

These tomatoes have been genetically engineered for better flavor and longer shelf life. Some scientists hope that genetic engineering will eliminate the proteins that cause food allergies, but others see problems with this approach.

The U.S. Food and Drug Administration consider GM foods safe, but some experts worry that they could cause problems for people with food allergies.

According to *Food Allergy News*:

> While the idea of having allergen-free food is appealing, there must be safety procedures incorporated into the production process to ensure that allergen-containing food is not confused or combined with allergen-free varieties. Additionally, . . . it may be impossible to avoid the possibility of plant cross breeding due to the natural environmental factors on the farm thus making it impossible to guarantee that crops are truly "allergen-free." The theory is a good one, but there are many problems to be addressed.[25]

Most of the research on allergen-free or less allergenic GM foods is taking place in the United States, Japan, and Australia. Ultimately, this technology could reduce or prevent severe allergic reactions for some individuals. But could this technology eliminate food allergy altogether?

"In reality, I don't think it will ever be feasible [for such plants] to be non-allergenic," says Dr. Wesley Burks, associate professor of pediatrics at the University of Arkansas for Medical Sciences and Arkansas Children's Hospital. He says:

> There are too many proteins in a peanut to either take the proteins out of the plant or alter them individually to make them non-allergenic. . . . I think it may be possible [for such plants to be made] less allergenic for some patients and that the less-allergenic plants might be used for future feeding to the population so we are less likely to develop the specific allergy in the first place. Any less-allergenic foods that will be produced and utilized in the food supply will need to be labeled appropriately.[26]

Food for Thought

These are exciting times for the area of food allergy education and research. While various organizations and individuals are educating others about the seriousness of food allergies, scientists are beginning to learn more about the complexities of the condition. They know more about how food allergies work and are coming closer to understanding how they develop.

Progress is also being made in the development of allergen-free foods, new drugs, and new therapies that eventually may lead to better treatment options, vaccines, and even a cure. Perhaps then, one day, fatal reactions to food allergies will be a thing of the past. And people with food allergies will no longer have to live with the constant fear of accidental exposure.

Chapter Notes

Chapter 1 What's the Deal With Food Allergies?

1. Author's interview with college student, Michelle Risinger, February 2005.

2. The Food Allergy and Anaphylaxis Network, "Food Allergies Now Believed to Affect 1-in-25 Americans According to FAAN Study Released at AAAAI Annual Conference, Americans with Seafood Allergies More Than Double Those with Peanut Allergies," press release, March 22, 2004, <http://www.food allergy.org/press_releases/seafoodpress.html> (August 6, 2004).

3. "Food Allergy Basics," *The Food Allergy and Anaphylaxis Network*, n.d., <http://www.foodallergy.org/media.html> (August 6, 2004).

4. "Tips to Remember: Food Allergy," *AAAAI Patients and Consumers Center*, n.d., <http://www.aaaai.org/patients/publiced mat/tips/foodallergy.stm> (August 7, 2004).

5. Ray Formanek Jr., "Food Allergies: When Food Becomes the Enemy," *Food and Drug Administration*, n.d., <http://www.fda.gov/fdac/features/2001/401_food.html> (August 7, 2004).

6. "New Allergies May Develop in Adults," *Nutrition Health Review*, Fall 2002, p. 8.

7. Author's query to Media Relations Department, The Food Allergy and Anaphylaxis Network, Fairfax, Virginia, 2005.

8. The Food Allergy and Anaphylaxis Network.

9. Formanek Jr.

10. Marianne S. Barber, *The Parent's Guide to Food Allergies: Clear and Complete Advice From the Experts on Raising Your Food-Allergic Child* (New York: Henry Holt and Company, LLC, 2001), p. 9.

11. "What are the most common food allergies?" *MedicineNet*, April 1, 2002, <http://www.medicinenet.com/food_allergy/page4.htm> (August 11, 2005).

12. Dr. Robert S. Zeiger, "A Member Asks . . . 'Does food allergy run in families?'" *Food Allergy News*, December 2002–January 2003, p. 5.

13. Chad K. Oh, M.D., *How to Live with a Nut Allergy: Everything You Need to Know If You Are Allergic to Peanuts or Tree Nuts* (New York: McGraw Hill, 2005), pp. 14–15 and 18–19.

14. Zeiger, p. 5.

15. Associated Press, "Transplant Recipient Gets Nut Allergy," *JS Online: Milwaukee Journal Sentinel,* January 27, 2003, <http://www.jsonline.com/alive/ap/jan03/ap-transplanted-a1012703.asp> (March 19, 2005).

Chapter 2 The Body's Response

1. Author's interview with Tracy Thayer, March 2005.

2. "Quick Reference: Peanuts, Folic Acid and Peanut Allergies," *March of Dimes,* n.d., <http://www.marchofdimes.com/professionals/14332_1819.asp> (February 23, 2005).

3. Marianne S. Barber, *The Parent's Guide to Food Allergies: Clear and Complete Advice From the Experts on Raising Your Food-Allergic Child* (New York: Henry Holt and Company, LLC, 2001), pp. 6–7.

4. Ibid.

5. "Anaphylaxis," *Medfacts: An Educational Health Series from National Jewish Medical and Research Center,* January 12, 2005, <http://www.njc.org/medfacts/anaphylaxis.html> (January 26, 2005).

6. "What is Anaphylaxis?" *Asthma and Allergy Information and Research (AAIR) Home Page,* n.d., <http://www.users.globalnet.co.uk/~aair/anaphylaxis.htm> (August 7, 2004).

7. Cameron Sew Hoy, "How people feel when they are about to have an anaphylactic reaction and what symptoms occur when this happens," *Anaphylaxis,* n.d., <http://www.users.bigpond.net.au/csewhoy/allergy.html> (August 7, 2004).

8. Ibid.

9. Ibid.

10. "Information about Anaphylaxis," *The Food Allergy and Anaphylaxis Network,* August 27, 2004, <http://www.foodallergy.org/anaphylaxis.htm> (January 23, 2005).

11. Author's interview with college student, Michelle Risinger, February 2005.

Chapter 3   Food Allergy Testing

1. Personal experience of author, Sherri Mabry Gordon, 2000–2001.
2. Chad K. Oh, M.D., *How to Live with a Nut Allergy: Everything You Need to Know If You Are Allergic to Peanuts or Tree Nuts* (New York: McGraw Hill, 2005), p. 31.
3. Marianne S. Barber, *The Parent's Guide to Food Allergies: Clear and Complete Advice From the Experts on Raising Your Food-Allergic Child* (New York: Henry Holt and Company, LLC, 2001), p. 17.
4. Johns Hopkins Medical Institutions, "Guidelines for food allergy testing," press release, July 7, 2004, <http://www.eurekalert.org/pub_releases/2004-07/jhmi-gff070604.php> (January 19, 2005).
5. John M. James, M.D., "Commonly Asked Questions About Food Allergy Testing," *Food Allergy News*, vol. 12, no. 3, February–March 2003, pp. 1, 9.
6. Ibid.
7. Ibid.

Chapter 4   A Closer Look at Food Allergens

1. Lee H. Freund, M.D. and Jeanne Rejaunier, *The Complete Idiot's Guide to Food Allergies* (New York: Alpha Books, 2003), p. 72.
2. Hugh A. Sampson, M.D., "Milk and Egg Allergies," *Food Allergy News*, June–July 2004, vol. 13, no. 5, pp. 1, 9.
3. Freund and Rejaunier, p. 73.
4. Sampson, pp. 1, 9.
5. Judy Tidwell, "An Immune System's Response to Milk Proteins," *Milk Allergy*, n.d., <http://allergies.about.com/cs/milk/a/aa082399.htm> (January 22, 2005).
6. Sampson, pp. 1, 9.
7. Ibid.
8. Marianne S. Barber, *The Parent's Guide to Food Allergies: Clear and Complete Advice From the Experts on Raising Your Food-Allergic Child* (New York: Henry Holt and Company, LLC, 2001), p. 57.

9. Ibid., p. 59.

10. Johns Hopkins Medical Institutions, "Researchers Close In on Source of Peanut Allergy," press release, November 22, 1996, <http://www.hopkinsmedicine.org/press/1996/NOVEMBER/19964.htm> (November 16, 2005).

11. American Academy of Allergy, Asthma and Immunology, "Major advances in peanut allergy research may bring hope to 1.5 million Americans," press release, July 10, 2003, <http://www.aaaai.org/media/news_releases/2003/07/071003.stm> (August 15, 2005).

12. "Research Update: Recurrent Peanut Allergy," *Food Allergy News*, December 2002–January 2003, vol. 12, no. 2, p. 13.

13. D. M. Fleischer, M. K. Conover-Walker, L. Christie, A. W. Burks, and R. A. Wood, "Peanut allergy: Recurrence and its management," *Journal of Allergy and Clinical Immunology*, November 2004, vol. 114, no. 5, pp. 1195–1201.

14. Author's query to Media Department, The Food Allergy and Anaphylaxis Network, 2005.

15. The Food Allergy and Anaphylaxis Network, "Food Allergies Now Believed to Affect 1-in-25 Americans According to FAAN Study Released at AAAAI Annual Conference, Americans with Seafood Allergies More Than Double Those with Peanut Allergies," press release, March 22, 2004, <http://www.food allergy.org/press_ releases/seafoodpress.html> (August 6, 2004).

16. Ibid.

17. Sampson, pp. 1, 9.

18. Ibid.

19. Freund and Rejaunier, p. 74.

20. Janice Vickerstaff Joneja, PhD, RDN, *Dealing with Food Allergies: A Practical Guide to Detecting Culprit Foods and Eating a Healthy, Enjoyable Diet* (Boulder, Colo.: Bull Publishing Company, 2003), p. 182.

21. Charlotte E. Grayson, MD, "Living with a Soy Allergy," *WebMD Health*, February 2004, <http://my.webmd.com/content/article/61/67476.htm> (January 23, 2005).

22. Joneja, p. 162.

23. "What is Celiac Sprue?" *Celiac Sprue Research Foundation*, n.d., <http://www.celiacsprue.org/celiacsprue.html> (March 10, 2005).

24. Bruce Sweet, M.D., "Oral Allergy Syndrome," *Bruce Sweet Allergy and Asthma*, 2005, <http://www.homestead.com/brucesweet allergyasthma/files/ORAL_ALLERGY_SYNDROME2005.htm> (August 11, 2005).

25. Heidi Knapp Rinella, "Fatal Reaction: When Dinner Turns Deadly," *Las Vegas Review-Journal*, August 11, 2004, <http://www.reviewjournal.com/lvrj_home/2004/Aug_11_Wed_2004/living/24346336.html> (August 11, 2005).

26. "Understanding Labels and Cross Contact," pamphlet, The Food Allergy and Anaphylaxis Network, Fairfax, Va., 2005, pp. 14–16.

Chapter 5   Living With Food Allergies

1. American Academy of Allergy, Asthma and Immunology, "New research on food allergy released at AAAAI Annual Meeting," press release, March 10, 2003, <http://www.aaaai.org/media/news_releases/2003/03/031003c.html> (January 24, 2005).

2. Author's interview with Anne Muñoz-Furlong, February 2005.

3. Ibid.

4. "The Impact of Food Allergy," *Allergy New Zealand Inc.*, May 2003, <http://www.allergy.org.nz/media/?issue=releases/1205case> (February 4, 2005).

5. Author's interview with Lisa Cipriano Collins, March 2005.

6. *Stories from the Heart: A Collection of Essays From Teens with Food Allergies*, vol. I (Fairfax, Va.: The Food Allergy and Anaphylaxis Network, 2000), pp. 27–28.

7. "The Impact of Food Allergy," *Allergy New Zealand Inc.*, May 2003, <http://www.allergy.org.nz/media/?issue=releases/1205case> (February 4, 2005).

8. Author's interview with Lisa Cipriano Collins, March 2005.

9. Anne Muñoz-Furlong, "Daily Coping Strategies for Patients and Their Families," *Pediatrics*, vol. 111, no. 6, June 2003, p. 1660.

10. Author's interview with Anne Muñoz-Furlong, February 2005.

11. Muñoz-Furlong.

12. Author's interview with Anne Muñoz-Furlong, February 2005.

13. American Academy of Allergy, Asthma and Immunology.

14. *Stories from the Heart: A Collection of Essays From Teens with Food Allergies*, vol. II (Fairfax, Va.: The Food Allergy and Anaphylaxis Network, 2002), pp. 63–65.

15. American Academy of Allergy, Asthma and Immunology.

16. Heidi Knapp Rinella, "Fatal Reaction: When Dinner Turns Deadly," *Las Vegas Review-Journal,* August 11, 2004, <http:// www.reviewjournal.com/lvrj_home/2004/Aug_11_Wed_2004/ living/24346336.html> (August 11, 2005).

17. Author's interview with Anne Muñoz-Furlong, February 2005.

18. Author's interview with Lisa Cipriano Collins, March 2005.

19. Christopher Weiss, Anne Muñoz-Furlong, Terence J. Furlong, and Julie Arbit, "Impact of Food Allergies on School Nursing Practice," *Journal of School Nursing,* October 2004, vol. 20, no. 5, pp. 268–278.

20. The Food Allergy and Anaphylaxis Network, "Study reinforces need for standardized food allergy guidelines and training in schools nationwide," press release, October 7, 2004.

21. Ibid.

22. Muñoz-Furlong, p. 1657.

23. "Students with Chronic Illnesses: Guidelines for Families, Schools, and Students," *National Heart, Lung, and Blood Institute,* n.d., <http://www.nhlbi.nih.gov/health/public/lung/asthma/ guidfam.pdf> (October 4, 2005).

24. "Airlines: Flying with a Peanut Allergy," *The Food Allergy and Anaphylaxis Network,* n.d., <http://www.foodallergy.org/Advocacy/ airlines.html> (August 6, 2004).

25. Author's interview with Michelle Risinger, February 2005

26. "Airlines: Flying with a Peanut Allergy."

27. "Travelers and Consumers: Prepare for Takeoff," *Transportation Security Administration,* 2005, <http://www.tsa.gov/public/display? content=09005198004a922> (August 12, 2005).

28. Ibid.

29. Phil Couvrette, Associated Press, "Boyfriend Unaware of Deadly Peanut Allergy," *Boston.com*, November 30, 2005, <www.boston.com/nbews/world/canada/articles/2005/11/30/boyfriend_unaware_of_deadly_peanut_allergy?mode=PF> (January 17, 2006).

30. "The Kiss of Death (or at least of allergic reaction)," *Consumer's Research Magazine*, vol. 85, no. 7, July 2002, p. 7.

31. Author's interview with Anne Muñoz-Furlong, February 2005.

32. Author's interview with Lisa Cipriano Collins, March 2005.

33. "Position Statement," *American Academy of Allergy, Asthma and Immunology*, 2005, <http://www.aaaai.org/media/resources/academy_statements/position_statements/ps34.asp> (August 16, 2005).

34. "Legislative and Advocacy Update," *Food Allergy News*, vol. 13, no. 1, October–November 2003, p. 10.

35. "Opinion on the Applicability of Federal Statutes to Private Schools," U.S. Department of Justice, Disability Rights Section, 1996.

36. Lisa Cipriano Collins, *Caring for Your Child With Severe Food Allergies* (New York: John Wiley & Sons, Inc., 2000), pp. 65–66.

37. *Stories from the Heart: A Collection of Essays From Teens with Food Allergies*, vol. II (Fairfax, Va.: The Food Allergy and Anaphylaxis Network, 2002), pp. 83–85.

Chapter 6 What Science Is Doing

1. *Stories from Parents' Hearts: Essays by Parents of Children with Food Allergies* (Fairfax, Va.: The Food Allergy and Anaphylaxis Network, 2001), p. 5.

2. Author's interview with Anne Muñoz-Furlong, February 2005.

3. Anne Muñoz-Furlong, "We're All in This Together!" *Food Allergy News*, December 2004–January 2005, vol. 14, no. 2, p. 2.

4. Bengt Björkstén, "Genetic and Environmental Risk Factors for the Development of Food Allergy," *Medscape*, 2005, <http://www.medscape.com/viewarticle/504850_print> (August 17, 2005).

5. American Academy of Allergy, Asthma and Immunology, "Research Reveals Genetic Link," *All About Allergies*, n.d.,

<http://allergies.about.com/cs/research/a/blpeanutgenetic.htm> (August 16, 2005).

6. Björkstén.

7. "Food Allergy Research: Cause, Treatment, and Cure," *Food Allergy News*, vol. 13, no. 2, pp. 1, 7.

8. Ibid.

9. "Vaccine, charcoal may treat peanut allergy," *The New Zealand Herald*, November 7, 2003, <http://www.nzherald.co.nz/story display.cfm?reportID=16&storyID=3512136> (August 16, 2005).

10. "Food Allergy Hope," *ScienCentral*, March 17, 2005, <http:// www.sciencecentral.com/articles/view.php3?type=article.article_id =218392504> (August 15, 2005).

11. "Vaccine, charcoal may treat peanut allergy."

12. Author's interview with Anne Muñoz-Furlong, February 2005.

13. "Anti-IgE Study Update," *Food Allergy Initiative*, n.d., <http:// www.foodallergyinitiative.org/section_home.cfm?section_id=3& sub_section_id=1&article_id=66&middle_link=1> (January 26, 2005).

14. "Positive Results of Anti-IgE Clinical Trial in Patients Suffering from Peanut Allergy Presented at AAAAI Conference," *PR Newswire*, March 10, 2003, <http://www.prnewswire.com/cgi-bin/stories.pl?ACCT=104&STORY=/www/story/03-10-2003/0001905220&EDATE=> (August 15, 2005).

15. Author's interview with Anne Muñoz-Furlong, February 2005.

Chapter 7 Food Allergies and the Future

1. Author's interview with Anne Muñoz-Furlong, February 2005.

2. National Restaurant Association, "National Restaurant Association Committed to Food Allergy Safety and Training," news release, May 2, 2002, <http://www.restaurant.org/press room/print/index.cfm?ID=406> (February 4, 2005).

3. "The Food Allergy Training Program for Restaurants and Food Services," *Food Allergy Initiative*, n.d., <http://www.foodallergy initiative.org/section_home.cfm?section_id=6&sub_section_id=4> (January 26, 2005).

4. Food Allergy & Anaphylaxis Network, "New Movie, *Monster-in-Law*, insensitive to millions of Americans with food allergies," press release, May 10, 2005, <http://www.foodallergy.org/press_releases/monsterinlaw.html> (August 20, 2005).

5. National Restaurant Association.

6. The Food Allergy and Anaphylaxis Network, "New Will Smith movie, *Hitch*, reveals common food allergy threat," press release, February 14, 2005, <http://www.foodallergy.org/press_releases/hitch.html> (August 20, 2005).

7. The Food Allergy and Anaphylaxis Network, "Arthur Cracks Open Peanut Allergies on PBS KIDS GO!" press release, April 2005, <http://www.foodallergy.org/press_releases/binkygoes nuts.html> (August 20, 2005).

8. Policy Statement, Walt Disney World, Media Relations Department, February 2005.

9. "Food Allergies: Health Data Fact Sheet," Center for Health Statistics, New Jersey Department of Health and Senior Services, 2005.

10. "Restaurant Advocacy," *The Food Allergy and Anaphylaxis Network*, n.d., <http://www.foodallergy.org/Advocacy/restaurants.html> (August 6, 2004).

11. The Food Allergy and Anaphylaxis Network, "Kids Nationwide Warding Off the Worst Scare of All this Halloween," news release, September 24, 2004.

12. Lisa Cipriano Collins, *Caring for Your Child With Severe Food Allergies* (New York: John Wiley & Sons, Inc., 2000), p. 76.

13. S. H. Sicherer, T. J. Furlong, J. DeSimone, and H. Sampson, "The U.S. Peanut and Tree Nut Allergy Registry: Characteristics of reactions in schools and day care," *National Library of Medicine,* April 2001, <http://www.ncbi.nlm.nih.gov> (December 19, 2005).

14. A. Nowak-Wegrzyn, M. K. Conover-Walker, and R. A. Wood, "Food-allergic reactions in schools and preschools," *National Library of Medicine*, July 2001, <www.ncbi.nlm.nih.gov> (December 19, 2005).

15. The Food Allergy and Anaphylaxis Network, "Kids encouraged to Be a Pal to those with food allergies," news release, August 16, 2004.

16. Ibid.

17. The Food Allergy and Anaphylaxis Network, "California students now allowed to carry life-saving medication," news release, September 30, 2004.

18. Author's interview with Anne Muñoz-Furlong, February 2005.

19. "Food Allergies," *Chain Leader*, November 2004, vol. 9, no. 12, p. S-7.

20. The Food Allergy and Anaphylaxis Network, "President Bush signs Food Allergen Labeling and Consumer Protection Act," press release, August 3, 2004, <http://www.foodallergy.org/press_releases/falcpasign.html> (August 6, 2004).

21. Ibid.

22. Ibid.

23. Australian Consumers' Association, "Allergies and food labels," n.d., <http://www.choice.com.au/viewarticleasonepage.aspx?id=101546&catId=100495&tid=100008&p=1> (October 21, 2005).

24. "Research Update: Genetically Engineered Allergen-Free Foods," *Food Allergy News*, Special Insert, April–May 2003.

25. Ibid.

26. "In the News: Allergy-Free Peanuts, Soybeans, Wheat, and Rice: A Possibility?" *Food Allergy News*, December 2002–January 2003, p. 6.

Glossary

anaphylaxis—A generalized allergic reaction that involves many systems of the body, including the heart, lungs, kidneys, and blood vessels, and can lead to death if not treated quickly.

biphasic reaction—An allergic reaction that returns two to three hours after the symptoms from the first reaction go away.

casein—The curd that forms when milk is left to sour.

coincidental allergies—Food allergies from different food families that are not related.

cross contact—A phenomenon that occurs when one food comes in contact with another food and their proteins mix, causing each food to then contain small amounts of the other food, even though it cannot be seen.

cross-reactivity—When an allergy to one member of a food family results in the person being allergic to all foods in the group.

diluent—A solution used to dilute something.

epinephrine—Also known as adrenaline, it is the drug of choice in treating an anaphylactic reaction.

EpiPen—Self-injection system that provides a dose of epinephrine to treat anaphylaxis. EpiPen Jr. is used for children.

flare—The red area surrounding the hive that appears during a skin prick test.

food allergen—The protein in a particular food that causes an allergic reaction.

food challenge—The only test that can determine allergies once and for all; consists of feeding a person small amounts of foods that he or she is allergic to as well as foods that are safe for him or her to eat (sometimes called the double-blind placebo-controlled food challenge).

food diary—A log of the dates, times, and foods a person eats over a period of time as well as symptoms he or she experiences.

food intolerance—A metabolic disorder that does not affect the immune system.

genetically modified foods—Sometimes called GM foods or GMOs (genetically modified organisms); foods that have been changed to produce desirable qualities such as resistance to disease or a lower ability to cause allergic reactions.

gluten intolerance—An intolerance for gluten, which is a complex mixture of proteins found in grains such as wheat, rye, and barley. Not a food allergy.

glycoprotein—A molecule that consists of a carbohydrate plus a protein.

histamines—Chemicals found in the body's cells that are responsible for allergic symptoms.

immune system—The part of the body that protects it from infection, germs, and disease.

immunoglobulin E (IgE)—Antibodies manufactured by the body to protect it from germs and infection.

lactose intolerance—An inability to digest milk products due to a lack of the enzyme (lactase) needed to digest milk sugar.

mast cell—A specific cell that is found in body tissues, especially the nose, throat, lungs, skin, and gastrointestinal tract. During an allergic reaction, the mast cell releases histamines and other chemicals.

metabolic disorder—An inability to metabolize, or break down, food.

oral allergy syndrome—A condition in which certain fresh fruits and vegetables cross-react with the pollens that cause hay fever; this can cause an allergic response in which people affected experience an itchy mouth or scratchy throat.

RAST (radioallergosorbent test)— A test that measures the blood to determine the level of IgE antibodies present and is used to predict the likelihood of a food allergy.

wheal—The hive that appears during a skin prick test.

whey—The watery part of milk that is left after the curd is removed.

For More Information

American Academy of Allergy, Asthma and Immunology
555 East Wells Street
Milwaukee, WI 53202
414-272-6071

American Academy of Pediatrics National Headquarters
The American Academy
  of Pediatrics
141 Northwest Point Boulevard
Elk Grove Village, IL 60007-1098
847-434-4000

American College of Allergy, Asthma and Immunology
85 West Algonquin Road,
Suite 550
Arlington Heights, IL 60005
708-427-1200

American Medical Association Chicago Headquarters
515 N. State Street
Chicago, IL 60610
312-464-5000

Asthma and Allergy Foundation of America
1233 20th Street NW, Suite 402
Washington, D.C. 20036
202-466-7643
1-800-727-8462

The Food Allergy and Anaphylaxis Network (FAAN)
11781 Lee Jackson Highway, Suite 160
Fairfax, VA 22033
1-800-929-4040

Food Allergy Initiative
237 Park Avenue, 21st Floor
New York, NY 10017
212-527-5835

Food and Drug Administration
5600 Fishers Lane
Rockville, MD 20857-0001
888-INFO-FDA (888-463-6332)

National Institute of Allergy and Infectious Diseases
Building 31, Room 7A-50
31 Center Drive MSC 2520
Bethesda, MD 20892-2520
301-496-5717

U.S. Department of Agriculture Food and Nutrition Information Center
301-436-7725

Further Reading

Books

Brynie, Faith Hickman. *1001 Questions About Your Immune System You Felt Defenseless to Answer . . . Until Now.* Brookfield, Conn.: Twenty-First Century Books, 2000.

Ford, Jean. *Breathe Easy! A Teen's Guide to Allergies and Asthma.* Broomall, Pa.: Mason Crest Publishers, 2004.

Hammond, Leslie, with Lynne Marie Rominger. *The Kid-Friendly Food Allergy Cookbook: More Than 150 Recipes That Are Wheat-Free, Gluten-Free, Dairy-Free, Nut-Free, Egg-Free, and Low in Sugar.* Gloucester, Mass.: Fair Winds Press, 2004.

Lennard-Brown, Sarah. *Allergies.* Chicago: Raintree, 2004.

Oh, Chad K. *How to Live with a Nut Allergy: Everything You Need to Know If You Are Allergic to Peanuts or Tree Nuts.* New York: McGraw Hill, 2005.

Stories from the Heart: A Collection of Essays from Teens with Food Allergies, Volume I. Fairfax, Va.: Food Allergy and Anaphylaxis Network, 2000.

Stories from the Heart: A Collection of Essays from Teens with Food Allergies, Volume II. Fairfax, Va.: Food Allergy and Anaphylaxis Network, 2002.

Internet Addresses

American Academy of Allergy, Asthma and Immunology
<http://www.aaaai.org>

Asthma and Allergy Foundation of America
<http://www.aafa.org>

Food Allergy and Anaphylaxis Network
<http://www.foodallergy.org>

Index